PENGUIN CLASSICS

AGRICOLA *and* GERMANIA

PUBLIUS (?) CORNELIUS TACITUS was born *c.* AD 56, perhaps in southern Gaul (modern Provence); his father was probably of equestrian rank. By 75 he was in Rome, where he trained as an orator and eventually embarked on a senatorial career; in 76 he married the daughter of the consul Cn. Julius Agricola, whose biography he would later write. His swift rise up the ladder of senatorial offices indicates the favour of the reigning emperors; he reached the pinnacle of the senatorial career when he held the consulship (97). Although he continued to hold public office, serving as proconsul of Asia (112/13), he also increasingly devoted himself to writing historical works: *Agricola* in 97–8, *Germania* in 98 and *A Dialogue concerning Orators* probably in the first decade of the next century. By *c.* 110 he had completed the first of his major works, *The Histories*, covering Roman history from 69 to 96; his second major work, *The Annals*, covered the period from 14 to 68. Tacitus probably lived into the reign of Hadrian (117–38), but there is no evidence for his later life or the date of his death.

HAROLD MATTINGLY was born at Sudbury, Suffolk, in 1884. After studying classics at Cambridge and Roman administrative history in Berlin and Freiburg, he took up a position in the department of printed books at the British Museum in 1910 and two years later was transferred to the department of coins and medals. He there began cataloguing the Museum's holdings in Roman imperial coinage, a project that ultimately resulted in two monumental and indispensable reference works: *Coins of the Roman Empire in the British Museum* (6 vols., 1923–62) and *Roman Imperial Coinage* (10 vols., 1923–81). Among his other important works was a series of articles that completely revised the chronology of Roman republican coinage. After retiring from the British Museum in 1948, he settled in Chesham, Buckinghamshire, where he died in 1964.

J. B. RIVES received his PhD in Classics from Stanford University (1990) and taught at Columbia University and at York University in Toronto before moving to the University of North Carolina at Chapel Hill, where he is Kenan Eminent Professor of Classics. He is the author of *Religion and Authority in Roman Carthage* (1995) and *Religion in the Roman Empire* (2007), as well as numerous articles on aspects of religion in the Roman world. He has also published a translation, with introduction and commentary, of Tacitus' *Germania* (1999) and, for Penguin Classics, has revised Robert Graves' translation of Suetonius, *The Twelve Caesars* (2007).

TACITUS

Agricola
Germania

Translated by HAROLD MATTINGLY
Revised with an Introduction and Notes by J. B. RIVES

PENGUIN BOOKS

PENGUIN CLASSICS

Published by the Penguin Group
Penguin Books Ltd, 80 Strand, London WC2R ORL, England
Penguin Group (USA) Inc., 375 Hudson Street, New York, New York 10014, USA
Penguin Group (Canada), 90 Eglinton Avenue East, Suite 700, Toronto, Ontario,
Canada M4P 2Y3 (a division of Pearson Penguin Canada Inc.)
Penguin Ireland, 25 St Stephen's Green, Dublin 2, Ireland
(a division of Penguin Books Ltd)
Penguin Group (Australia), 250 Camberwell Road, Camberwell, Victoria 3124, Australia
(a division of Pearson Australia Group Pty Ltd)
Penguin Books India Pvt Ltd, 11 Community Centre, Panchsheel Park,
New Delhi – 110 017, India
Penguin Group (NZ), 67 Apollo Drive, Rosedale, North Shore 0632, New Zealand
(a division of Pearson New Zealand Ltd)
Penguin Books (South Africa) (Pty) Ltd, 24 Sturdee Avenue, Rosebank, Johannesburg 2196, South Africa

Penguin Books Ltd, Registered Offices: 80 Strand, London WC2R ORL, England

www.penguin.com

This translation first published 1948
Revised translation published 2009

014

Translation copyright © the Estate of Harold Mattingly, 1948, 1970
Revisions to the translation and editorial material copyright © J. B. Rives, 2009
All rights reserved

The moral right of the copyright-holders has been asserted

Set in Postscript Adobe Sabon
Typeset by Macmillan Publishing Solutions
www.macmillansolutions.com
Printed in England by Clays Ltd, St Ives plc

ISBN: 978-0-140-45540-3

www.greenpenguin.co.uk

Contents

Abbreviations

Roman Praenomina

A.	Aulus
C.	Gaius
Cn.	Gnaeus
L.	Lucius
M.	Marcus
P.	Publius
Q.	Quintus
Ser.	Servius
Sex.	Sextus
T.	Titus
Ti.	Tiberius

Frequently Cited Ancient Authors and Works

Caes.	Julius Caesar
Civ.	*The Civil War*
Gall.	*The Gallic War*
Dio	Cassius Dio, *History*
Diod. Sic.	Diodorus Siculus, *Historical Library*
Juv.	Juvenal, *Satires*
Livy	Livy, *History of Rome*
Mela	Pomponius Mela, *Geography*
Plin.	Pliny (the Elder)
NH	*Natural History*
Plin.	Pliny (the Younger)
Ep.	*Epistles*
Pan.	*Panegyric*

Ptol.	Ptolemy, *Geography*
Strabo	Strabo, *Geography*
Suet.	Suetonius
Aug.	*Divus Augustus*
Calig.	*Gaius Caligula*
Claud.	*Divus Claudius*
Dom.	*Domitian*
Vesp.	*Divus Vespasian*
Vit.	*Vitellius*
Tac.	Tacitus
Agr.	*Agricola*
Ann.	*Annals*
Dial.	*A Dialogue concerning Orators*
Germ.	*Germania*
Hist.	*Histories*
Vell. Pat.	Velleius Paterculus, *History*

Collections of Inscriptions and Papyri

AE	*L'Année épigraphique* (Paris: 1888–)
CIL	Mommsen, T., et al., eds., *Corpus Inscriptionum Latinarum* (Berlin: 1863–)
ILS	Dessau, H., ed., *Inscriptiones Latinae Selectae* (Berlin: Weidmann, 1892–1916)
RIB	Collingwood, R. G., and R. P. Wright, eds., *The Roman Inscriptions of Britain* (Oxford: Clarendon Press, 1965–95)
TV	Bowman, A. K., and J. D. Thomas, eds., *The Vindolanda Writing Tablets* (*Tabulae Vindolandenses*), vols. 2 and 3 (London: British Museum Press, 1994–2003)

Chronology

BC

c. 386 Gauls sack Rome.

279 Gauls sack Delphi.

191 The Romans conquer Cisalpine Gaul.

121 The Romans establish a province in southern Transalpine Gaul.

113 The Romans first encounter the Cimbri, who defeat an army under Cn. Papirius Carbo.

107 The Tigurini, allies of the Cimbri, defeat L. Cassius Longinus.

105 The Cimbri and their allies defeat M. Aurelius Scaurus, Q. Servilius Caepio and Cn. Mallius Maximus.

104–100 C. Marius consul; decisively defeats the Teutones (102) and the Cimbri (101).

58–50 Julius Caesar in Gaul.

58 Caesar defeats first the Helvetii and then Ariovistus and his Germani.

55 Caesar crosses the Rhine into Germania and invades Britannia.

54 Caesar invades Britannia for the second time. M. Licinius Crassus invades Parthia.

53 Caesar crosses the Rhine for the second time. Crassus and his army massacred by the Parthians.

52 Caesar faced with major uprising in Gaul.

49–45 Roman civil wars between Caesar and his opponents.

44 The assassination of Caesar (15 March) sparks off another series of civil wars.

41–40 The Parthian prince Pacorus invades Roman territory; is defeated by P. Ventidius Bassus.

38? The Ubii relocate to the Roman side of the Rhine.

31 Octavian (Augustus) defeats Mark Antony and Cleopatra at the Battle of Actium (2 September) to become the sole ruler of the Roman empire.

16–15 Augustus' stepsons Tiberius and Drusus conquer the Alpine regions and push back the Roman frontier to the upper Danube.

12–9 Tiberius campaigns in Pannonia and Moesia, Drusus campaigns in Germania. Drusus' naval expedition in the North Sea.

9 Drusus dies on the march back from the Elbe; is posthumously awarded the name Germanicus, which is inherited by his son.

8–7 Tiberius campaigns in Germania.

AD

4–6 Tiberius campaigns in Germania.

6–9 Tiberius suppresses revolt in Pannonia.

9 Germanic troops under Arminius massacre P. Quinctilius Varus and three legions at the Teutoburg Forest; Augustus brings frontier back to the Rhine.

10–11 Tiberius campaigns in Germania.

14–16 Drusus' son Germanicus campaigns in Germania.

14 Death of Augustus (19 August); Tiberius becomes emperor.

37 Death of Tiberius (16 March); Gaius (Caligula) becomes emperor.

39–40 Gaius campaigns in northern Europe.

40 Birth of Agricola (13 June).

41 Murder of Gaius (24 January); Claudius becomes emperor.

43 Claudius initiates conquest of Britannia with four legions (II Augusta, IX Hispana, XIV Gemina and XX Valeria) under command of A. Plautius.

43–7 A. Plautius governor of Britannia.

44 Claudius celebrates a triumph for his conquest of Britannia; names his son Britannicus.

47–52 P. Ostorius Scapula governor of Britannia; initiates advance into Wales. Founding of Roman colony at Camulodunum.

50 The town of the Ubii is made a Roman colony under the name Colonia Claudia Agrippinensis.

51 Cartimandua of the Brigantes turns over the Britannic resistance leader Caratacus to the Romans.

52–7 A. Didius Gallus governor of Britannia.

54 Death of Claudius (13 October); Nero becomes emperor.

56 Birth of Tacitus (?).

57–8 Q. Veranius governor of Britannia.

58–61 C. Suetonius Paulinus governor of Britannia.

60–61 Agricola serves in Britannia as military tribune. Revolt of Boudicca. Agricola returns to Rome, marries Domitia Decidiana.

61–3 P. Petronius Turpilianus governor of Britannia.

62 Birth and death of Agricola's first son.

63–4 Agricola serves in Asia as quaestor under L. Salvius Otho Titianus; birth of his daughter.

63–9 M. Trebellius Maximus governor of Britannia.

66 Agricola serves in Rome as tribune of the people. Nero withdraws Legio XIV Gemina from Britannia. Suicide of P. Clodius Thrasea Paetus.

68 Agricola serves in Rome as praetor. Revolt against Nero is suppressed, but Nero panics and commits suicide (9 or 11 June); Galba becomes emperor. In Britannia, M. Roscius Coelius, the legate of Legio XX Valeria, incites a mutiny against the governor Trebellius Maximus.

69 Murder of Galba (15 January); Otho becomes emperor. Civil wars between Otho and Vitellius; murder of Agricola's mother. Suicide of Otho (c. 16 April); Vitellius becomes emperor. More troops withdrawn from Britannia. Civil wars between Vitellius and Vespasian. C. Julius Civilis instigates a revolt among the Batavi. Murder of Vitellius (20 or 21 December); Vespasian becomes emperor, with C. Licinius Mucianus as his representative in Rome.

69–71 M. Vettius Bolanus governor of Britannia. Brigantes revolt against their queen Cartimandua. Legio XIV returns to Britannia, but shortly thereafter permanently withdrawn.

70 Agricola conducts levy of troops and is later appointed legate of Legio XX Valeria in Britannia. Revolt of the Batavi

suppressed by Q. Petilius Cerialis. Vespasian arrives in Rome (late summer).

71–3 Petilius Cerialis governor of Britannia; subdues the Brigantes. Legio II Adiutrix transferred to Britannia.

73 Agricola returns from Britannia; is enrolled among the patricians.

74–6 Agricola serves as governor of Aquitania.

74–7 Sex. Julius Frontinus governor of Britannia; completes subjugation of the Silures in southern Wales.

75 Execution of C. Helvidius Priscus.

76 Agricola serves as suffect consul; gives his daughter to Tacitus in marriage; is appointed governor of Britannia and made a pontifex.

77 Agricola arrives in Britannia in midsummer; defeats the Ordovices in northern Wales and subdues the island of Mona in late summer. Roman campaigns against the Bructeri lead to the capture of Veleda.

78 Agricola's second year in Britannia; campaigns in the north.

79 Agricola's third year in Britannia; overruns territory up to the Forth–Clyde isthmus and penetrates as far north as the Tay. Death of Vespasian (23 June); Titus becomes emperor.

80 Agricola's fourth year in Britannia; secures the territory up to the Forth–Clyde isthmus.

81 Agricola's fifth year in Britannia. Tacitus quaestor (?). Death of Titus (13 September); Domitian becomes emperor.

82 Agricola's sixth year in Britannia; begins the drive into Caledonia. Birth of his second son. Cohort of Usipi serving in Britannia mutiny and circumnavigate the island.

83 Agricola's seventh year in Britannia. Death of his second son. Battle of Mons Graupius. Agricola's fleet rounds the north of Britannia and overruns the Orkneys. Domitian campaigns against the Chatti; celebrates triumph.

84 Agricola recalled from Britannia in the spring and given triumphal honours.

85 Dacians invade Moesia and defeat the Roman army there.

86 Domitian drives Dacians back over the Danube; celebrates triumph. His general Cornelius Fuscus invades Dacia, but is defeated and killed.

87 Legio II Adiutrix transferred from Britannia to the Danube; the legionary fortress under construction at Inchtuthil in Caledonia is abandoned and the Roman frontier is pulled back.

88 Tacitus praetor.

89 Domitian makes peace with the Dacians; he attacks the Marcomani, Quadi and Iazyges, but is defeated. Domitian puts down the revolt of L. Antonius Saturninus, commander of the Roman army along the upper Rhine, and defeats his allies the Chatti; celebrates double triumph over the Chatti and the Dacians.

c. 90 Agricola is excused from the governorship of Africa or Asia. Domitian organizes the new provinces of Upper and Lower Germania.

92 The Iazyges invade Pannonia and destroy a legion; Domitian defeats them.

93 Death of Agricola (23 August); Tacitus returns to Rome after an absence of three or four years. Trial of Baebius Massa. Executions of Q. Junius Arulenus Rusticus, Herennius Senecio and the younger Helvidius; exile of Junius Mauricus; expulsion of philosophers from Rome.

96 Assassination of Domitian (18 September); Nerva becomes emperor. Trajan appointed governor of Upper Germania.

97 Roman nobles exiled by Domitian return to Rome. A Roman commander installs a new king over the Bructeri. Nerva adopts Trajan (late October). Tacitus suffect consul; begins *Agricola* (autumn).

98 Death of Nerva (27 January); Trajan becomes emperor. Tacitus completes *Agricola*; writes *Germania*.

101–2 Trajan's first war against the Dacians.

105–6 Trajan's second war against the Dacians; Dacia annexed as a province.

104–10 Tacitus writes *The Histories* and *A Dialogue concerning Orators* (?).

112/13 Tacitus proconsul of Asia; at work on *The Annals* (?).

117 Death of Trajan (11 August); Hadrian becomes emperor.

122 Fortifications along the Tyne–Solway line ('Hadrian's Wall') mark the limit of Roman control in Britannia.

Introduction

A. Rome, the Emperor and the Peoples of Northern Europe

A1. *Agricola* is a tribute to an admired father-in-law, whose greatest accomplishment was his role in the Roman conquest of Britain, and *Germania* is a description of the peoples who lived beyond the Rhine and the upper Danube, the boundaries of the Roman empire in western Europe. These two short works, dating to AD 97–8,[1] were the first historically oriented compositions of Tacitus, who would go on to become one of the greatest historians of ancient Rome. Despite their differences, the works share two themes, and it is this, as well as their brevity and their date of composition, that causes them so often to be printed together. The more obvious theme is the relationship between the Roman empire and the peoples of northern Europe, in the regions that the Romans called Britannia and Germania. Less obvious, but equally important, is the role that the conquest of these regions played in promoting, justifying and lending prestige to the system of one-man rule in Rome that historians describe as the principate or, less precisely, the empire. In order to understand these themes and the role they play in Tacitus' works, some historical background is necessary.

One of the defining events in early Roman history, and one that acquired an almost mythic status in the Romans' own conception of their past, was the sack of Rome in *c.* 386 BC by a band of invaders from over the Alps. The Romans, adapting the word that these people used for themselves, called them Galli or, in the English form of the name, 'Gauls' (Greek-speakers preferred the name 'Celts'). Soon afterwards others appeared in the region north of Greece, and in the following century bands of Gauls sacked the holy site of Delphi and invaded Asia Minor, settling in an area that eventually became known as Galatia. All these events made a huge impression, but for the Romans, of course, the sack of their own city was by far the most significant. For centuries it remained the only occasion on which a foreign enemy had succeeded in plundering the city of Rome. Many of these Gauls settled in the Po valley in northern Italy, a region that became known as Gallia Cisalpina, or 'Gaul this side of the Alps', and over time the Romans became more familiar with them; by the beginning of the second century BC, they had even brought Cisalpine Gaul under Roman rule. By the latter part of that century, largely because of their need for secure land routes to their possessions in Hispania, the Romans had also established control over the southern part of Gallia Transalpina, 'Gaul across the Alps'; this region became known as the Province, whence modern 'Provence'. Yet the 'Gallic terror', the fear of invasion by northern barbarians, remained a potent cultural force, and received a fresh impetus at the end of the second century BC with the appearance of new groups of northern barbarians, the Cimbri and Teutones, who again seemed poised to invade Italy. It was in order to counter this threat that the Roman people elected the great general C. Marius to an unprecedented five consulships in a row.

A2. Having successfully deflected the Cimbric threat, in the mid first century BC the Romans returned to the offensive. At the beginning of his proconsulship in Gaul in 58 BC, Julius Caesar embarked on a series of military interventions that quickly resulted in the Roman conquest of all Transalpine Gaul up to the Rhine and the English Channel; from this time on, 'Gaul' came increasingly to refer to Transalpine Gaul in particular. Caesar's motivations for this conquest are clear enough: he needed military glory, vast wealth and a personally loyal army in order to compete successfully in the power politics of the late Roman Republic. He obtained all these things in the course of his eight years of campaigning in Gaul, and they were what allowed him to defeat his enemies in the Roman civil wars of the 40s BC and establish himself as the sole ruler of the Roman world. But if his main motivations for the conquest concerned his own needs and ambitions, his presentation of it capitalized on the long-standing 'Gallic terror'; indeed, as the nephew by marriage of C. Marius, he could not have failed to observe how Marius' defence of Italy against the threat of northern invaders had won him an unprecedented position in Rome. It is thus not surprising that when the Helvetii, a people living in what is now western Switzerland, threatened to migrate into western Gaul, Caesar justified his attack on them by likening them to the Cimbri. He did the same with a group of Germani, who under their leader Ariovistus had crossed the Rhine and settled in eastern Gaul. It was the involvement in Gallic affairs that resulted from his campaigns against these two peoples that set the stage for his further conquest of Gaul.

In the course of this conquest, Caesar also initiated the first direct Roman contact with Britannia and Germania. In 55 BC he first crossed the Rhine into Germania, and then crossed the Channel and invaded Britannia. He followed up the latter with a larger-scale invasion of Britannia in 54 BC, and in the following year made another brief incursion into Germania. In both cases it seems that a major concern was prestige: Caesar was able to present himself as taking the glory of the Roman name into far distant and previously unknown territory. This was especially true in the case of Britannia. The early Greeks had thought that the earth was encircled by a huge river that they called Okeanos, 'Ocean'. Although several centuries of exploration meant that by Caesar's day the name 'Ocean' had become attached more prosaically to the great sea beyond Europe, it nevertheless still carried strong connotations of its mythic origins; by invading Britannia, therefore, an island actually in the Ocean, Caesar could legitimately claim to have taken Roman arms to the ends of the earth. In practical terms, it is not entirely clear what Caesar intended to achieve with his two invasions of Britannia. The fact that at the end of his second campaign he took hostages and imposed tribute on Britannic leaders suggests that he intended to bring the region under direct Roman rule. In the event, however, this did not happen.

Caesar's attention was called back first to Gaul, where increasing discontent led to a large-scale uprising in 52 BC, and then to Rome, where growing friction with his chief rival and some-time ally Cn. Pompeius eventually resulted in civil war. Britannia remained free of Roman rule, although the southeastern part of the island was from that time onwards firmly within the sphere of Roman influence.

In contrast to his invasions of Britannia, Caesar's expeditions across the Rhine were not intended to be anything more than brief displays of force. In *The Gallic War*, the account that he wrote of his conquest of Gaul, his whole treatment of the Germani is meant to emphasize their wildness and ferocity; he presents them not as potential subjects of Rome, like the Gauls and even the Britanni, but rather as a threat that must be kept back on their side of the Rhine. Caesar seems to have been the first Greek or Roman writer to present the Rhine as the natural boundary between the Gauls and the Germani; indeed, we may go further and say that Caesar is the first extant writer to present the Germani as a separate people, a large-scale ethnic grouping of the same order as the Gauls but entirely distinct from them. Archaeological and linguistic research has shown that the cultural situation in northern Europe was in fact highly complex, and that the Rhine did more to connect than to separate the peoples who lived on its banks. But a simple division between Gauls and Germani served Caesar's purposes more effectively than the complex reality. If the Rhine was the natural border between two distinct peoples, then Caesar could present any movement across it as an invasion like that of the Cimbri fifty years before, and himself, consequently, as the new Marius, warding off the invaders from Italy. Likewise, if the Rhine was a natural border, Caesar could justify his claim to have conquered an entire nation, 'all of Gaul'. Not everyone accepted Caesar's new ethnography of Europe, with its fundamental distinction between Gauls and Germani; many Greek writers continued to refer indiscriminately to all the peoples of northern Europe as Celts. But Caesar's eventual successor, Augustus, did accept it, and through him it became an established part of the Roman conception of the world.

A3. The Roman civil wars of the 40s and 30s BC meant that for a number of years no Roman leader followed up on Caesar's ventures into Britannia or Germania. But after these wars had at last come to an end, Caesar's adopted son, Octavian (or Augustus, as he came to be called), who had emerged as sole ruler of the Roman world, began to turn his thoughts to the peoples at the northern edges of the empire. The laudatory poetry from the early part of his reign is filled with allusions to his future conquests, which would extend the boundaries of the empire to the ends of the earth; the close connection between military achievement and political domination that was so apparent in the career of Caesar continued to hold true for Augustus. There is some evidence that early in his reign Augustus may have contemplated a renewed invasion of Britannia, although in the end he was content to promote Roman interests there through diplomatic means. Germania, however, was another story.

In the early part of the second decade BC, Augustus embarked on an ambitious plan to extend Roman rule in Europe far beyond its previous boundaries. He began in the years 16–15 BC, when his stepsons Tiberius and Drusus conquered the Alpine regions and pushed back the frontier to the upper Danube. Tiberius was then sent to campaign in Pannonia and Moesia, where he established the lower Danube as the new boundary of the Roman empire, while Drusus was assigned to Germania. In 12 BC, Drusus led Roman armies across the Rhine; he campaigned in Germania for four years, finally reaching the Elbe in 9 BC but dying on his march back. The Senate, in recognition of his achievement, awarded him the posthumous victory-name 'Germanicus', which passed to his elder son. Roman campaigns in Germania continued after Drusus' death, and were placed under the direction of Tiberius himself in 4–6. At this point, however, Augustus' plans began to go awry. First, in 6 a major revolt broke out in Pannonia, taking Tiberius away from Germania. His replacement there was P. Quinctilius Varus, who seems to have focused more on organizing Germania as a Roman province than on continuing the military campaigns. Someone, however, had seriously misjudged the situation. In 9 a large number of Germanic troops under the command of their leader

Arminius ambushed Varus and his army in the Teutoburg Forest, massacring three legions almost to a man. It was the worst Roman military disaster in decades, and Augustus, already an old man, never recovered from the blow. Tiberius was brought in to stabilize the situation, but his campaigns in 10–11 and those of Drusus' son Germanicus in 14–16 were clearly intended only to stabilize the situation and help restore Rome's reputation; the plan to turn Germania into a Roman province was permanently abandoned.

A4. Despite Tiberius' extensive military experience, or perhaps because of it, throughout his reign as emperor he steadfastly maintained Augustus' posthumous advice not to extend the boundaries of the empire. His successor Gaius, however, had other ideas. Unlike Tiberius, he did not come to the throne with an already established military reputation, something that, as should by now be apparent, was crucial to a Roman emperor's overall prestige. Moreover, as the son of Germanicus and the grandson of Drusus, he may well have felt some pressure to live up to his family's reputation; even his nickname Caligula, by which he is now better known, was one that he had acquired as a little boy accompanying his father during the Germanic campaigns of 14–16. Gaius certainly seems to have planned some sort of major initiative in northern Europe, although it is difficult to get a clear sense from the scanty and hostile sources of what precisely he did or hoped to accomplish. We do know that, after massive military preparations, he spent some nine months in Gaul in 39–40; he seems first to have campaigned in Germania, and then perhaps to have laid the groundwork for an invasion of Britannia. But whatever Gaius may have intended, in the end he seems actually to have accomplished little or nothing.

Gaius was succeeded by his uncle Claudius, who likewise came to the throne in urgent need of notable military accomplishments to bolster his authority. But Claudius turned his back on his family's long connection with Germania and instead revived Caesar's plan to conquer Britannia. Planning began within two years of his accession, and the invasion itself took place probably in the early summer of 43. The forces employed were considerable: four legions (Legio II Augusta, IX Hispana, XIV Gemina and XX Valeria) and a large number of auxiliary units, under the general command of A. Plautius. Claudius himself took part in the campaign, but only for sixteen days, in order to preside over the Roman army's triumphant entry into Camulodunum (modern Colchester), the main town in southeastern Britannia. The details of the conquest are uncertain, since the ancient narrative sources are incomplete and the archaeological evidence is difficult to date with precision. It is nevertheless clear enough that the Roman advance was swift, so that by 47, when Plautius turned over command to his successor, much of what is now southern and central England seems to have been under some form of Roman domination; the first Roman settlement, a colony of veterans at Camulodunum, was probably founded before the end of the decade. In some areas, for example that of the Iceni in what is now East Anglia, the Romans preferred alliances to outright conquest, allowing the native peoples to retain their local rulers. It was one of these allied rulers, Cartimandua of the Brigantes in present-day Yorkshire, who in 51 turned over to the Romans the great leader of native resistance to the conquest, Caratacus. With the capture of Caratacus, Claudius evidently decided that enough had been achieved to justify the construction of a triumphal arch in Rome; an inscription that apparently adorned the arch praises Claudius 'for receiving in surrender eleven kings of the Britanni, defeated without any loss, and being the first to bring the barbarian peoples across the Ocean under the sway of the Roman people' (*ILS* 216). Perhaps even more significantly, he had already bestowed upon his son a new victory-name, Britannicus, a deliberate replacement for the name Germanicus, which for so long had held such glamour for his family.

A5. When Nero succeeded Claudius in 54, he maintained the policy of extending Roman control in Britannia. The area of modern Wales was a particular focus of military activity, while in the north Cartimandua continued to be a loyal ally, despite unrest among her people. But in 60 disaster struck. While the

governor C. Suetonius Paulinus was in northern Wales, attempting
to subjugate the island of Mona (modern Anglesey), the Iceni,
under their queen Boudicca, rose in revolt. Together with their
allies, they sacked the colony at Camulodunum as well as settlements at Londinium (London) and Verulamium (St Albans) and
defeated the attempts of nearby Roman authorities to put down
the rebellion. Suetonius was eventually able to defeat the enemy,
resulting in the suicide of Boudicca, but unrest clearly continued.
For the rest of the 60s, the Roman advance in Britannia seems
largely to have come to a standstill. Tacitus, in his account of this
period, attributes this to a lack of initiative on the part of the
governors (*Agr.* 16), but there must have been a need for considerable retrenchment and rebuilding after the revolt of Boudicca.
Moreover, in about 66 Nero withdrew one of the four legions,
XIV Gemina, for use in a proposed campaign in the East. It is
likely enough that the lack of further Roman aggression in
Britannia during the 60s resulted from deliberate imperial policy.

In the spring of 68 the governor of Gallia Belgica challenged
Nero's rule, and although his revolt was put down by L. Verginius
Rufus, the commander of the Roman legions along the upper
Rhine, it set in motion a series of civil wars and short-lived
emperors that ended only with the accession of Vespasian in
December 69. These upheavals affected almost every part of the
empire. In Britannia, although Legio XIV Gemina returned in
69, it was almost immediately transferred to the Rhine and never
returned; another 8,000 troops departed to support the short-
lived emperor Vitellius. At the same time, the Brigantes rose up
against their pro-Roman queen Cartimandua, and the legate of
Legio XX Valeria, after a falling out with the governor Trebellius
Maximus, incited his troops to mutiny. Along the Rhine, the situation was even worse. Initially pretending to aid the cause of
Vespasian, C. Julius Civilis, a leader of the Germanic Batavi,
stirred up a major rebellion of native peoples in northeastern
Gaul; after considerable successes, the rebels were finally defeated
in 70 by Vespasian's general Q. Petilius Cerialis.

A6. Once Vespasian had consolidated his position, however, he
turned his attention to the northern frontiers. On the continent,

he seems to have authorized the first expansion of Roman power across the Rhine since the days of Augustus. This did not involve a major war of conquest, but rather the strategic occupation of territory along the Germanic bank of the upper Rhine. Vespasian also revived the expansionist policy in Britannia. After Petilius Cerialis' success in putting down the revolt of Civilis, Vespasian appointed him governor and sent with him the recently formed Legio II Adiutrix, bringing the total number of legions in Britannia back up to four. Cerialis and his successors, Julius Frontinus and Tacitus' father-in-law Agricola, were able to complete the subjugation of Wales, deal with the Brigantes and push Roman control into what is now lowland Scotland. There is some reason to think that Titus, who succeeded his father in 79, may have decided on a frontier at the Forth–Clyde isthmus; if he did, however, his decision was reversed by his brother Domitian, who succeeded him in 81.

Like Gaius and Claudius before him, Domitian came to power in the shadow of his father's and brother's military accomplishments, and like them he seems from an early date to have sought opportunities to acquire military glory of his own. In Britannia he apparently authorized Agricola's drive beyond the Forth–Clyde isthmus into Caledonia, and in Germania he initiated a major campaign against the Chatti in 83. The latter he treated as a great success, celebrating a triumph and adopting the name Germanicus; he even reorganized Roman territory along the Rhine into two new provinces that he named Upper and Lower Germania. All this was apparently meant to demonstrate that he had at long last achieved the long-standing Roman goal of conquering Germania. Tacitus and Pliny, writing shortly after Domitian's death, dismissed his accomplishments there with utter scorn, and it is certainly true that he did not actually conquer Germania. Nevertheless, he did extend Roman rule further into the region beyond the upper Rhine and Danube, a territory that by Tacitus' day was known as the decumate lands (see *Germ.*, n. 80).

By the mid 80s, however, Domitian had turned his attention further east, after the Dacians had crossed the lower Danube into Moesia and defeated the Roman army stationed there.

This was the first of a long series of wars along the Danube that not only occupied the rest of Domitian's reign but also resulted ultimately in Trajan's conquest of Dacia early in the second century. This shift of focus to the Danube meant that Britannia and the Rhine received correspondingly less attention. In 86 or 87 Domitian instituted a gradual withdrawal of Roman forces from the north of Britannia and transferred Legio II Adiutrix to the Danube, thereby permanently reducing the number of legions in Britannia to three. By the reign of Trajan, the Roman frontier had been brought back to the Tyne–Solway line, which Trajan's successor Hadrian caused to be fortified with the famous wall that goes by his name. Apart from the reoccupation of lowland Scotland for about twenty-five years in the mid second century and the emperor Septimius Severus' campaigns in the highlands in the early third century, Hadrian's Wall remained the boundary of Roman rule in Britannia. In Germania, Trajan built upon his predecessors' advance into the decumate lands in order to establish a solid frontier connecting the upper Rhine and Danube, but there was no further attempt to extend Roman rule beyond the Rhine. When Tacitus was writing *Agricola* and *Germania* in 97–98, however, these long-term developments were not yet apparent.

B. Tacitus' Life and Works

B1. Our sources of information for Tacitus' life are meagre: a few brief allusions in his own works and in the letters of the younger Pliny, and two inscriptions, one incomplete and the other a tiny fragment. Nevertheless, we can deduce from these some of the main outlines of his life and career. Tacitus himself says that his *dignitas*, public standing, was initiated by Vespasian, augmented by Titus and further advanced by Domitian (*Hist.* 1.1.3). Most scholars take this to mean that Vespasian granted him the right to hold senatorial office, and that accordingly Tacitus was by birth of equestrian rather than senatorial status. By chance, the elder Pliny mentions a Cornelius Tacitus who served as procurator in Gaul, probably in the late 40s or early 50s (*NH* 7.76); since 'Tacitus' is a rare cognomen and the only other known 'Cornelius Tacitus' is the historian, it is likely that this procurator was his father or possibly uncle. A few hints in our sources suggest that the family originated in what had been Cisalpine Gaul or, perhaps more likely, in Gallia Narbonensis, the old 'Province' of Transalpine Gaul; the fact that Tacitus was to contract a marriage connection with Agricola, whose family originated at Forum Julii in Narbonensis, lends some weight to the latter hypothesis.

His full name was probably Publius Cornelius Tacitus. The praenomen is that given by the oldest manuscript of Tacitus' works; the fifth-century poet Sidonius Apollinaris calls him Gaius (*Epistles* 4.14.1 and 22.2), but he may have misremembered his sources. A small fragment of an epitaph from Rome that has recently been reinterpreted as belonging to the historian (*AE* 1995, no. 92 = *CIL* VI.41106) suggests that the name 'Tacitus' was followed by an additional name beginning with 'C', perhaps 'Caecina'. His date of birth must be inferred from his later political career and his own vague remarks about his age at various points of his life; the year 56 is most likely, although 57 or even 58 are also possible. By 75 he was in Rome, attending the leading orators of the day (*Dial.* 1–2); he must have been a young man of considerable promise, since the following year Agricola, who as consul had just reached the top of the political ladder, judged him a suitable husband for his daughter (*Agr.* 9). Certainly from the very beginning his public career was marked by signs of imperial favour. The fragmentary epitaph reveals that his first public position was as *decemvir stlitibus iudicandis*, a member of the Board of Ten for Trying Lawsuits, a minor magistracy that involved presiding over court cases; minor magistracies of this sort were the normal preliminary to a senatorial career, and the one held by Tacitus was one of the more prestigious. He is then likely to have served as a tribune of the soldiers, the usual next step in a public career. No evidence survives concerning Tacitus' tribuneship, but A. R. Birley has made the attractive suggestion that he might have served in Britannia under his father-in-law Agricola.[2] He next acted as *quaestor Augusti*, as we know from the epitaph. The quaestorship was the office that brought admission to the Senate; the fact that Tacitus was one of the two quaestors out of twenty who were assigned to the emperor himself is another mark of favour. This office he probably held in 81, under Titus, which would fit with his remark that his public standing had been augmented by that emperor.

Under Domitian, Tacitus continued his climb up the ladder of senatorial offices. We know from his own evidence (*Ann.* 11.11.1) that in 88 he was praetor; more significantly, he was also *quindecimvir sacris faciundis,* a member of the Board of Fifteen for Conducting Rituals, one of the major public priesthoods of Rome. This was a remarkable honour for someone of equestrian background and only thirty or so years of age. Because these priesthoods were few in number and held for life, openings were infrequent and competition for them was intense; Tacitus must have been chosen over the heads of older and more distinguished men. After his praetorship, Tacitus spent three or four years away from Rome (*Agr.* 45), presumably in one of the provincial offices normally assigned to senators of praetorian standing. He seems to have returned to Rome in the autumn of 93, shortly after Agricola's death. In the latter part of 97 he served as suffect consul, and while in office gave the funeral oration for L. Verginius Rufus, the general who almost thirty years previously had put down the first revolt against Nero (Plin. *Ep.* 2.1.6).

We know from Pliny that Tacitus had long been one of the leading orators of Rome; Pliny claims that when he was 'just a boy' he chose Tacitus as his model (*Ep.* 7.20.4), even though Tacitus was his senior by only five or so years. The third of Tacitus' short works, *Dialogus de oratoribus* or *A Dialogue concerning Orators*, is evidence of his deep interest in oratory, in both its aesthetic and social aspects. Its date has been the subject of much dispute; a few scholars have suggested that it is a work of Tacitus' youth, but the majority place it somewhere in the period 104–10. Pliny addressed a number of his published letters to Tacitus, and the two seem to have had a fairly close association, at least as regarded literary matters. A couple of years after Tacitus' consulship, he and Pliny were joint prosecutors in one of the celebrated trials of the day, that of a notoriously corrupt provincial governor (Plin. *Ep.* 2.11.2). By that time, however, the focus of Tacitus' literary interests had shifted. His funeral oration for Verginius Rufus may have made him think of the oration that he had not been able to deliver at his father-in-law's funeral. At any rate, it seems that he was already at work on *Agricola* in the autumn of 97 (*Agr.* 3 with n. 7), a task that apparently occupied him into the following year (*Agr.* 44 with n. 102). He followed it with *Germania*, also written in 98 (*Germ.* 37 with n. 97), and not much later embarked on his first major historical work, conventionally known as *The Histories*. His joint prosecution with Pliny shows that he continued to take an active part in public life, and an inscription reveals that he eventually served as proconsul of Asia, probably in 112/13;[3] nevertheless, in his later years his efforts must have been largely focused on writing history.

B2. In the preface to *Agricola*, Tacitus announced that in his next work he would record 'the servitude we once suffered and . . . the blessings we now enjoy' (*Agr.* 3), which most people have interpreted as plans to write an account of the reigns of Domitian and Nerva. What he ended up writing, however, was something rather different. *The Histories* was a large-scale work in either twelve or perhaps fourteen books that covered the history of Rome from 1 January 69 to the assassination of Domitian in September 96; the first four books and a bit of the fifth are all that survive, taking the story down only to the early months of 70. We know from letters that his friend Pliny wrote to supply him with material (*Ep.* 6.16 and 20, 7.33) and that he was at work on it in the period 105–7, but we can only conjecture when precisely he began and finished it; most scholars date it generally to the period 104–10.

For his *magnum opus*, conventionally known as *The Annals*, we have even less to go on. Indeed, the inscription recording his proconsulship of Asia is the last datable reference to Tacitus, so that it is impossible to do more than guess when he died. The general tendency is to assume that he was already at work on *The Annals* by the time he was proconsul of Asia and that he lived, and continued working on it, into the reign of Hadrian. *The Annals* was an even more ambitious work than *The Histories*.

It originally consisted of eighteen or perhaps sixteen books, beginning with the accession of Tiberius in 14 and ending with the fall of Nero in 68. Whether it bridged the gap between Nero's death in early June 68 and the start of the year 69, where *The Histories* begins, is not known, since only parts of the work have survived: Books 1–6, with the exception of most of 5 and a bit of 6, covering the reign of Tiberius, and Books 12–15, together with the latter half of 11 and the first half of 16, covering the end of Claudius' reign and the beginning of Nero's.

The Histories and *The Annals* are among the great masterpieces of Latin literature. In them, Tacitus was concerned above all to analyse the effect that the absolute power of the emperors had on Roman politics, society and culture, and his analysis was largely a negative one. Imperial power, as he saw it, resulted in the corruption of both ruler and ruled, breeding secrecy, paranoia, cruelty and moral dissipation in the emperors themselves, and hypocrisy, subservience, cowardice and greed in their subjects. He certainly looked back with longing to the glory days of the Republic, when there was liberty at home and imperial expansion abroad. Yet he never indulged in simpleminded nostalgia: he knew that there was no going back, and that the institution of the principate was as necessary as it was corrosive. The question was how best to respond to it, how to live with integrity and contribute to the public good amidst the power, corruption and lies of imperial Rome. The answer, for himself, was to become a historian. In *The Histories* and *The Annals*, Tacitus pushes the Latin language further than any prose writer had done before in order to penetrate beneath the secrecy and misrepresentations of Roman imperial history and reveal the underlying tyranny and servility for what they were. Although this agenda reaches its fullest expression in the major works of his maturity, we can trace its origins to *Agricola*.

C. *Agricola*

C1. In spite of its brevity and apparent simplicity, *Agricola* is a complex and often surprising work. One issue that has generated much scholarly discussion is that of determining its genre.

It is most easily and most frequently described as a biography of Agricola, and that description, as far as it goes, is certainly correct; indeed, the full Latin title of the work is *De vita Iulii Agricolae* or *On the Life of Julius Agricola*. The problem is that it does not go very far. Anyone who reads *Agricola* with care notices very quickly, if not always fully consciously, that it is a biography of a rather unusual sort. On the one hand, it is curiously lopsided: Agricola's seven years as governor of Britannia receive much more detailed treatment than the rest of his life, and over half of that narrative is devoted to an account of a single battle. On the other hand, it contains a fair amount of material that is only tangentially related to Agricola himself: a description of Britannia and a brief history of Roman rule there, a digression about a famous event that took place while Agricola was governor. The following outline of the work, based on the traditional chapter numbers, will serve to bring out some of its unusual features.

1–3: Preface
4–9: Life of Agricola up to the governorship of Britannia
(AD 40–76)
10–17: Background to Agricola's governorship of Britannia
   10–12: Ethnography of Britannia
   13–17: Survey of the Roman conquest of Britannia
18–38: Agricola's governorship of Britannia
   18–27: Agricola's first six years as governor (AD 77–82)
   28: Digression: mutiny of Usipi
   29–38: Agricola's seventh year as governor: Battle of Mons Graupius (AD 83)
      29: Introduction
      30–32: Speech of Calgacus
      33–4: Speech of Agricola
      35–8: Description of the battle
39–43: Agricola's recall from Britannia, last years and death
(AD 84–93)
44–6: Conclusion

One way to account for the work's odd shape is to argue that Tacitus' real goal was not so much to give a balanced general account of Agricola's life as to highlight his virtues and accomplishments. He therefore focused on Agricola's greatest achievement, his governorship of Britannia and his role in its conquest. Agricola certainly extended the Roman occupation of Britannia further north than anyone had ever done before and indeed, although Tacitus could not have known it, further than anyone would do after as well. In order to emphasize Agricola's achievements in Britannia, then, Tacitus deliberately skimmed over the rest of his life and career while at the same time including background information about Britannia that would set Agricola's accomplishments there in higher relief.

A further point should be kept in mind as well. In Graeco-Roman antiquity, biography was not a fixed and stable genre. On the contrary, it took a number of different forms and tended to merge into other genres: history, antiquarianism, even oratory. It is not unreasonable to think of *Agricola* as in some respects a substitute for the funeral oration that Tacitus, had he been able, would no doubt have delivered for his father-in-law. Such speeches were expected not simply to provide an overview of the deceased's life, but more importantly to praise him. As we have seen, this is precisely what Tacitus does in *Agricola*. Again and again he omits precise details, and instead elaborates on Agricola's virtues in highly rhetorical, and often highly conventional, terms. A related genre whose influence is apparent especially in the conclusion is the consolation, a speech or essay intended to comfort the survivors of the deceased. Here too praise played a part, although the emphasis was on relieving the grief of the mourners. Hence we find Tacitus waxing eloquent about Agricola's good fortune in dying before the worst excesses of Domitian's tyranny and exhorting his wife and daughter to take him as a model for their own lives.

Another genre that impinges deeply on *Agricola* is history. A number of the work's apparently peculiar features are in fact standard conventions of ancient historiography. The description of Britannia, for example, follows a well-established pattern of including ethnographic digressions within larger historical works; previous examples in Latin literature occur in the works of Caesar and Sallust, and the tradition ultimately extends back to the very 'Father of History', Herodotus (see further section D1 of the Introduction). The same is true of Tacitus' elaborate handling of the Battle of Mons Graupius, with its paired speeches by the opposing generals, its vivid and detailed account of the battle and its careful enumeration of the dead; abundant parallels for all these features can be found in Livy, Caesar and many earlier historians, and Tacitus would eventually employ them at greater length in his full-scale historical works. Indeed, some scholars go so far as to describe *Agricola* as a sort of preliminary exercise, a vehicle for trying his hand at the techniques he would need in the future. There is perhaps something to this idea, but it would be a mistake to press it too hard and downplay the significance of *Agricola* as a fully realized work on its own terms.

C2. Tacitus' primary goal was of course to praise Agricola; there is no need to question his sincere admiration for his father-in-law. But he also develops a number of other themes, many of which recur in his later works as well. One of these is a concern with Roman imperial expansion. This is something that Tacitus clearly endorsed. Throughout *Agricola* there is an implicit assumption that the proper task for Roman generals and armies is the defeat of new enemies and the conquest of new lands (see especially *Agr.* 13, 16–17 and 24). Most modern historians would agree that Domitian showed good sense in pulling back from Agricola's conquests in Caledonia: not only must it have become clear that the resources required for a permanent occupation would be far in excess of any benefit that would accrue, but the troops were more urgently needed elsewhere. For Tacitus, however, the policy was simply a reflection of Domitian's jealousy and resentment; he sums up his view in his preface to *The Histories* by tartly observing that 'Britannia was thoroughly conquered and immediately abandoned' (*Hist.* 1.2). The same bitterness over Roman failure to follow through with a conquest shows up again in *Germania*. At the same time, however, Tacitus is no simple-minded champion of Roman imperialism. He several times voices his opinion that the changes brought by Roman rule are as much to the bad

as to the good (for example, *Agr.* 11, 16 and 21), and displays
a talent for vividly representing the grievances of native peoples
against Roman expansion. Indeed, perhaps the most memorable line in the entire work sums up how outsiders might have
viewed the conquests of the Romans: 'they create desolation
and call it peace' (*Agr.* 30).

As I noted above, another important theme, and one of
immediate concern to Tacitus personally, was how a person
living under a tyranny could best serve the public good. It is
striking how close the figure of Domitian comes to dominating
the text: his presence looms in the background of the preface,
despite his being unnamed, and at the end he is almost more of
a focus than Agricola. Tacitus himself of course had a very successful public career under Domitian, but his experience of that
emperor's duplicity and paranoia, especially in the latter part of
his reign, clearly scarred him deeply. One episode in particular,
I believe, played a crucial part in shaping Tacitus' project in
Agricola, and deserves detailed consideration.

In the autumn of 93, it seems, not long after Tacitus returned
to Rome from his service in the provinces, a series of treason
trials took place in the Senate. The defendants were a group of
Roman nobles tied together by kinship and common ideals. The
origins of this group lay with a senator named Thrasea Paetus,
who had opposed the Senate's acquiescence in the tyrannical
behaviour of Nero, been tried for treason and forced to commit
suicide in 66. He was survived by his wife Arria and daughter
Fannia; the latter was married to another senator, Helvidius
Priscus, who, following the lead of his father-in-law, similarly
opposed Vespasian and was eventually put to death in 75. These
men had their admirers: under Domitian, the senator Arulenus
Rusticus wrote a laudatory account of Thrasea Paetus, and
Herennius Senecio did the same for Helvidius Priscus, with the
help of Priscus' widow Fannia. For reasons that remain obscure,
Domitian became suspicious of these men and everyone associated with them. The charges against Rusticus and Senecio
apparently centred on their accounts of Thrasea and Priscus;
charges were also brought against Priscus' son Helvidius (for
casting veiled aspersions on Domitian in a stage farce), his widow

Fannia (for helping Senecio with his biography), Fannia's mother Arria and Rusticus' brother Mauricus and wife Gratilla. Rusticus, Senecio and the younger Helvidius were put to death, the rest sent into exile. (For the details, see further *Agr.* 2 with nn. 3 and 6, and *Agr.* 45 with nn. 103–5.) Since Tacitus' friend Pliny had close connections with the entire group, it is likely that Tacitus also knew them, perhaps quite well. After the assassination of Domitian in September 96, the survivors were free to return from exile, and seem to have been back in Rome by early 97. Their return must have prompted Tacitus to think anew about the trials in which they had been involved, and when he began working on *Agricola* later that year the issues that emerged out of this episode were clearly much on his mind. As always with Tacitus, his reactions were complex.

On the one hand, he seems to have felt that the sort of ostentatious opposition to the principate represented by this group was possibly self-promoting and certainly useless. As admirable as their ideals might have been in the abstract, their actions in fact achieved little more than the increase of their own fame. For Tacitus, the proper response to a tyrant like Domitian was not defiance, but a continued willingness to do one's duty to the commonwealth as best one could. The qualities that he emphasizes in *Agricola* are accordingly *moderatio* and *prudentia*, *obsequium* and *modestia*, restraint and good sense, duty and discretion. His model was not Thrasea Paetus or Helvidius Priscus, but rather his own father-in-law Agricola, who achieved great things as long as Domitian allowed him to, and then refused to kick against the pricks once he had been recalled (*Agr.* 42). As several scholars have pointed out, Tacitus' highly successful public career suggests that he too had chosen duty and discretion over ostentatious opposition, and some have even suggested that *Agricola* was primarily intended as an apologia for his own involvement in public life under Domitian. This, I think, is too simplistic a view, but it remains true that Tacitus does advocate a particular solution to the challenge of being a good man under a bad emperor.

On the other hand, what seems to have disturbed Tacitus most about the trials of Rusticus and his fellows was not so

much Domitian's power over people's lives, but his power over
their thoughts. When he first refers to those trials (*Agr.* 2), the
thing that he really emphasizes is the public burning of Rusticus'
and Senecio's works. Although Tacitus was not an uncritical
admirer of Thrasea Paetus and Helvidius Priscus, this attempt
to suppress their stories must have struck him as part of a larger
and more systematic attempt on the part of the emperors to
control information and to repress the free exchange of ideas,
to ensure that the only available narrative of the principate was
the one that the emperors themselves propagated. There were
other aspects to this attempt as well, such as the habitual secret-
iveness and duplicity of emperors like Domitian, who always
tried to hide their real thoughts and motivations, so that one
never knew where one stood (*Agr.* 39 and 42). There were likewise the secret schemes devised by the emperors and their
personal advisers, rumoured but impossible to verify (*Agr.* 40).
There was above all the danger of informers, and the conse-
quent need to watch one's own speech and to be wary of reveal-
ing one's true thoughts and opinions; in the preface to *Agricola*,
Tacitus stresses that this constant repression meant that people
gradually lost their ability not only to speak freely but even to
think freely (*Agr.* 3). The lesson that Tacitus seems to have
drawn from the trials of Rusticus and his associates was thus
that resistance to tyranny was most useful, and most necessary,
when it took the form of challenging these attempts to control
speech and thought and memory. It was as a historian, not as a
public figure, that Tacitus continued the work of the senatorial
opposition. It was his conviction that the historian, even if he
could never recover the full truth, could at least expose the
distortions produced by tyrannical power. As we have seen, it
was this conviction that gives the works of his maturity so
much of their force, and it was in writing *Agricola* that he first
engaged with it.

C3. It should by now be clear that Tacitus' goals in *Agricola*
were not identical with those of a modern historian; it should
accordingly come as no surprise that he does not always satisfy
the expectations that we bring to modern historical works. For

one thing, we rarely find the level of detail in *Agricola* that we would like. Although Tacitus names each of Agricola's predecessors, he describes their activities in the most general terms, not so much summarizing their accomplishments as presenting them as foils for Agricola. He rarely mentions specific places or peoples or native leaders by name, even those that in his day were very familiar. Perhaps most vexing for modern historians is his disinclination to provide specific dates. Apart from the dates of Agricola's birth and death (*Agr.* 44), he avoids them entirely, providing at most vague indications like 'then', 'the following year', or 'immediately afterwards'. As a result, the chronology of Agricola's consulship and subsequent governorship of Britannia is uncertain. The traditional dating is that he was consul late in 77, and served as governor 78–84; in more recent years, however, there has been growing support for dating the consulship to 76 and the governorship to 77–83, and that is the dating I have followed here.[4]

Other sources of information allow us to fill in some of the details that Tacitus did not care to supply. In *The Histories* and *The Annals*, Tacitus himself provides more thorough accounts of some events to which in *Agricola* he simply alludes in passing. There is likewise the voluminous Roman history of Cassius Dio, written some one hundred years after Tacitus, even though parts of it survive only in brief excerpts and epitomes. Suetonius' biographies of the emperors from Caesar to Domitian tend to be rich in details like names and memorable anecdotes, although Suetonius is more likely simply to list events than to narrate them. Documentary sources also shed some light. Agricola himself appears in a small handful of inscriptions, such as those on a pair of lead pipes from the legionary fortress at Chester that were made in 79 and name him as governor (*RIB* 2.2434.1–3), and more can be linked to other people or specific events mentioned by Tacitus. Of particular interest are the Vindolanda tablets, several hundred wooden writing tablets discovered in the 1970s and 1980s at the Roman fort of Vindolanda near Hadrian's Wall. These date to between *c.* 90 and 120, somewhat after the time of Agricola, and include a wide range of personal letters and military reports. As fascinating as they are, however, they rarely contain material with much specific relevance to Agricola. Lastly, there is abundant archaeological evidence. Both amateurs and professionals have been studying the remains of Roman Britain for centuries, and over the years numerous forts and military posts have been linked to Agricola. In many cases, however, these are difficult to date very precisely on purely archaeological grounds, and hence their association with Agricola sometimes involves a certain amount of circular argumentation.

Careful study of other sources confirms that *Agricola* involves the sorts of biases we might expect: Tacitus tends to downplay the accomplishments of Agricola's predecessors in Britannia, to exaggerate Agricola's own accomplishments and to present Domitian in the worst possible light. For all that, it remains an invaluable source of information about Roman Britain. In reading it, however, we must remember that Tacitus did not write it for that reason. It was instead a literary composition, a vehicle for meditations on tyranny and reactions to it, and above all a tribute to a man whom he deeply admired and respected. It is in light of these goals that we should judge its quality.

D. *Germania*

D1. When we read *Agricola*, we have from the start a clear idea of the author's reasons for writing the work and of the particular concerns and issues that he had in mind during its composition; Tacitus himself provides an account of all this in the preface. When we read *Germania*, by contrast, we are entirely on our own. The work's full Latin title, *De origine et situ Germanorum* or *On the Origin and Location of the Germani*, does give some idea of the work's contents, but only of its first few chapters. Beyond that, Tacitus chose to leave the reader without any guidance at all, neither a preface nor even a conclusion: he begins by plunging right into the topic and ends when he has exhausted it. The effect is so odd that for a time some scholars thought that the work was actually written for inclusion within a larger historical work, much as Tacitus included an account of Britannia in *Agricola*. But it is difficult to see how a writer like

Tacitus, who in his larger works is so concerned with structure and balance, could have incorporated such a long study of the Germani into another project, and virtually no one today regards that as a serious possibility. Yet the lack of authorial guidance remains a striking feature of the text, and has led to long-standing debates over its meaning and significance.

The genre, at least, is clear enough: *Germania* is what scholars conventionally call an ethnography. Although the word itself is a modern coinage, despite its Greek roots, it is a useful designation for a well-established Greek and Roman literary tradition of describing foreign peoples. This tradition seems to have begun around 500 BC with the Greek writer Hecataeus of Miletus, who in his *Periegesis*, literally 'a leading around', presented an account of the world as it was known in his day. Although we know the work only from brief quotations in later writers, it seems that Hecataeus wrote as if conducting the reader on a journey from place to place, pausing to provide information about regional boundaries, the origins and customs of the inhabitants and other items of interest. Later writers developed the precedent set by Hecataeus along three different lines. Some continued with the format of the periegesis, compiling itineraries of particular regions or even, as Hecataeus himself did, the whole of the known world. Others abandoned the periegetic framework and expanded the discussion of individual peoples or regions, writing what we might call ethnographic monographs. Still others incorporated smaller-scale ethnographies within historical works. The key figure here is Herodotus, who in his account of the wars between the Persians and Greeks provided descriptions, sometimes very extensive, of the various peoples in the Persian empire; it was this tradition of incorporating ethnographic digressions into historical works that Tacitus followed in *Agricola*, as I noted above in section C1.

Tacitus' *Germania*, along with the description of India written a generation or so later by Arrian, is the only ancient ethnographic monograph to survive complete. But there are enough ethnographic sections within extant historical works that we can get a fairly clear sense of the conventions of Graeco-Roman ethnography. There was for one thing a fairly standard set of topics. The most important of these concerned the actual people in question: there was usually some discussion of their origins (often framed in terms of their being either natives or immigrants), always a description of their physical characteristics, and normally some examination, with varying amounts of detail, of their religious, social and military customs. There was also almost always some discussion of their territory, including its borders, topography, climate and resources. In addition, there were various interpretative schemes that served to 'explain' the physical and behavioural characteristics of particular populations by reference to external phenomena such as the climate and the influences of the heavenly bodies. The architect Vitruvius, for example, writing in the reign of Augustus, explained that the peoples of the north, as a result of the moisture and cool climate, are large and fair, with red hair and blue eyes, whereas those of the south, where it is hot and dry, are small and dark, with curly hair and black eyes. Since heat makes the blood thin, southerners are resistant to heat but are cowardly; northerners, in contrast, cannot endure heat but are very brave. Likewise, the thin atmosphere of the south renders its inhabitants quick-witted, but the cold mists of northern climes produce a mental sluggishness. Vitruvius patriotically concludes that the people of Italy, situated at the perfect mean between these two extremes, have the best qualities of both (*On Architecture* 6.1.3–11). This one example is sufficient to show that these interpretative schemes functioned in effect to confirm and rationalize Graeco-Roman stereotypes about other peoples; although some elements in these stereotypes presumably had a basis in actual observations, others were obviously the result of cultural prejudices.

The conventions of the Graeco-Roman ethnographic tradition clearly shaped Tacitus' ideas when he was writing *Germania*, in terms of what he omitted as well as what he included. The most striking omission is of anything that we might properly describe as historical data. In *Agricola*, as we have seen, Tacitus followed his description of Britannia with a concise account of the Roman conquest. There is nothing like this in *Germania*; only in a single paragraph (*Germ.* 37) does Tacitus recount Roman interactions with the Germani, and even there he provides not so much a survey as a list, meant to underscore his point that the Germani are the most formidable of all Rome's opponents. As for what *Germania* includes, the following outline will show how far Tacitus followed ethnographic conventions in terms of topics.

1–27: The Germani in general
   1: Boundaries of Germania
   2–4: Origin of the Germani
   5–15: Customs of the Germani: public institutions
   16–27: Customs of the Germani: private life
28–46: Individual Germanic peoples
   28–37: Peoples beyond the Rhine
   38–46: Peoples beyond the Danube: the Suebi

It is clear that Tacitus dutifully covered all the conventional topics. It is equally clear, however, that in deciding on the overall structure of his work Tacitus was anything but conventional. The work falls into two sharply distinguished halves, to which Tacitus himself explicitly calls attention (*Germ.* 27): a description of the Germani in general, followed by a survey of the individual Germanic peoples. In effect, Tacitus combined an ethnography with a periegesis, a combination for which we have no parallel from antiquity.

D2. The identification of *Germania* as part of the ancient ethnographic tradition helps us to understand many aspects of the text, but it does not answer the questions posed by the lack of a preface. Why did Tacitus write this work? And why, if he wanted to write an ethnography, did he choose to write about the Germani in particular? As with *Agricola*, some scholars have suggested that it was a kind of preliminary exercise, intended to give Tacitus practice with a type of writing that he would need as a full-fledged historian. And as with *Agricola*, even though there may be something to this suggestion, it does little to help us to understand the text itself. A better approach is to begin with the fact that Tacitus apparently wrote *Germania* immediately after he finished *Agricola*. Since we may reasonably assume that he would have chosen his next topic with the idea of exploring further some of the themes and concerns that he had touched on in *Agricola*, we may consider whether any of these reappear in *Germania*.

As I noted in the previous section, one important theme that emerges in *Agricola* is a concern with Roman imperialism and its limits. Tacitus clearly regarded Domitian's decision to pull back from Agricola's conquests in Caledonia as a glaring example of the failure to achieve the conquests proper to Rome. Indeed, he went so far as to explain Domitian's alleged hostility to Agricola as arising from jealousy: Agricola's very real victories in Britannia made his own claims to have conquered Germania seem hollow. Some scholars have accordingly argued that *Germania* was deliberately intended as a companion piece to *Agricola*, so that just as the latter presented the real achievements of Agricola, so too the former would demonstrate in detail just how hollow Domitian's claims actually were. *Germania* certainly makes it obvious that the Germani remained unconquered, and on at least one occasion Tacitus gets in a very clear dig at Domitian, even though he does not name him (see *Germ.* 37 with n. 106; see also 29 with n. 80). Yet as an overall explanation for the text this interpretation is not very satisfactory, since it does little to account for its richness and variety of detail. Other scholars have proposed that Tacitus had a more immediately practical purpose. The new emperor, Trajan, was a man with a proven military track record, and was at that very time serving as governor of Upper Germania. Perhaps *Germania* was Tacitus' way of suggesting that the time had come at last to make good the hollow claims of Domitian and complete the one great enterprise abandoned by Augustus; perhaps he even meant it as a sort of intelligence report, to help facilitate the final conquest of Germania. There is possibly something to this suggestion, given the lengths to which Tacitus goes to emphasize the Germanic threat (see *Germ.* 37 in particular). But as I argued above, Tacitus seems to have felt quite strongly that the proper role of a historian was not to grandstand on current political debates but to provide insight into the past. In attempting to understand *Germania*, then, it is to the empire's past, and not to its future, that we should look.

If Tacitus, as a historian, was indeed interested in the limits of Roman imperialism, as *Agricola* seems to indicate, then it was only natural that his thoughts would have turned to Germania. As I indicated in section A of this Introduction, the Germani had for almost a century marked the limits of Roman imperialism, and had served repeatedly as the acid test for the ambitions of Rome's emperors. In *Germania*, Tacitus explores the reasons for this situation by analysing the character of the Germanic people. As he explicitly states, their resistance to Roman rule derived its force from their strong attachment to freedom: 'The freedom of Germania is a deadlier enemy than the despotism of Arsaces' (*Germ.* 37 with n. 99). But in Tacitus' view the Germani take their devotion to liberty too far, and refuse to endure any restraints. They arrive at assemblies whenever they choose, and their leaders must rely on persuasion and charisma, since they have no authority to command (*Germ.* 7 and 11). The key social relationships in Germanic society are based not on legal and social structures, but on emotions and voluntary personal ties; hence, Tacitus presents as its core institution the warrior band consisting of a leader and his followers (*Germ.* 13–15). As a result of their excessive freedom, the Germani are incapable of the discipline that the Romans had always regarded as the hallmark of their own virtue. On Tacitus' analysis, then, the greatest strength of the Germani is also one of their major weaknesses.

Another theme apparent in *Agricola* that also comes to the fore in *Germania* is that of civilization and its corrupting influence. The stereotypes of the ethnographic tradition made the Germani a perfect vehicle for exploring this topic further. Tacitus depicts the Germani as a kind of 'noble savage', free from the vices that civilization brings. Greed and luxury are virtually unknown among them: they have no interest in precious metals (*Germ.* 5), they know nothing about legacy-hunting and usury (20 and 26), they eat plain food (23) and have plain funerals (27). Likewise, they take sexual morality and child-rearing very seriously (*Germ.* 18–20), quite unlike, Tacitus implies, his fellow Romans. In all these respects, Tacitus seems to present the Germani as upholding the sort of strict and old-fashioned morality that the Romans believed their own ancestors observed.

D3. The subject of *Germania*, then, allowed Tacitus to meditate on a number of issues that had emerged in *Agricola* as particular areas of concern to him: Roman imperialism and its failures, freedom and its proper limits, civilization and morality. Most of its modern readers, however, have been less interested in pondering these themes than in exploiting the text as a source of information about the ancient peoples of northern Europe. This, of course, raises another key question about this text: how reliable is Tacitus' account? The question has been much debated. Scholars of the late nineteenth and early twentieth centuries tended to treat *Germania* almost as though it were the product of modern anthropological research. They expended considerable effort in correlating Tacitus' comments both with the evidence of later Germanic texts and traditions and with the findings of archaeological research in northern Europe. They accepted his enumeration of peoples in the second half of the work as a more or less comprehensive account, and carefully distributed the names he provides onto maps, associating them whenever possible with distinctive types of pottery or weaponry. In English scholarship, the high-water mark of this sort of approach was the commentary by J. G. C. Anderson, who insisted that 'so far as archaeological investigation can check its statements, the objective value of the *Germania* has, on the whole, been vindicated in a remarkable way by the research of recent times'.[5] In more recent times, however, the optimistic assumptions of scholars like Anderson have come under attack. Archaeologists are now much less confident that we can or even should identify particular clusters of distinctive artefacts with the tribal names supplied by Greek and Roman writers. For their part, historians and literary scholars now stress the highly rhetorical nature of the text and the pervasive influence within it of ethnographic stereotypes. This new emphasis has resulted in a much deeper understanding of these stereotypes and of Tacitus' use of them to pursue his particular interests. But it has also led some scholars to regard *Germania*

as virtually unusable as a source of reliable information about
the early peoples of northern Europe. The truth, in my view,
probably lies somewhere in the middle of these two extremes,
although perhaps closer to the latter than to the former.

There are certainly significant problems with regarding the
material in *Germania* as simply straightforward observation.
Indeed, Ronald Syme, perhaps the greatest Tacitean scholar of
the twentieth century, proposed that Tacitus took most of his
material from a single written source that he 'copied very closely'
and failed in many places to update.[6] But so dismissive an
assessment is probably unfair. For one thing, it is not clear that
Germania was as out of date as Syme thought: since Tacitus,
as I indicated above, chose to follow the conventions of the
ethnographic genre and to disregard the chronological dimen-
sion entirely, his failure to refer explicitly to recent developments is not significant. Nor is it by any means certain what
Tacitus' single written source could have been, since his survey
of Germanic peoples often shows striking divergences from the
extant accounts of other writers such as Strabo, Mela, Pliny and
Ptolemy. It is far more likely that he drew on a range of sources:
literary (earlier histories and geographies), documentary
(reports of merchants and scouts) and even oral; Tacitus may
very well have served on the Germanic frontier himself, and
certainly would have had many opportunities to talk both with
Romans who had experience of Germania and with Germani
serving in the Roman army. If this is the case, however, we need
to be cautious in assessing Tacitus' information, since we must
assume that beneath the smooth and consistent surface of the
text there lies a welter of sources that varied greatly in focus,
reliability and date.

The more substantial problems lie not so much with Tacitus'
immediate sources of information as with the initial sources.
How did the Romans know anything about the peoples of
Germania at all? With respect to those who lived near the Roman
frontier, it was easy enough, since multiple points of contact
existed: there was an extensive and steadily increasing cross-
border trade, there had been numerous Roman military operations in Germanic territory, there were numerous Germani who

served with the Roman army as auxiliaries or worked in the empire as slaves. Information about these peoples would have been fairly abundant and in some ways reasonably accurate, and it is likely that the fairly full general account of the Germani in the first half of *Germania* is informed largely by what the Romans knew of the Germani immediately across the Rhine and Danube. For more distant peoples, however, opportunities for obtaining data would have been strictly limited. Although some information might derive fairly directly from long-distance traders or more far-flung expeditions, much of it must surely have been at third or fourth hand, stories and rumours that reached Roman ears through a series of intermediaries. The possibilities for distortion in such a situation are obvious.

But even in the case of nearby peoples it would be a mistake to think in terms of pure and unbiased information. The ethnographic stereotypes that I touched on above were not merely a literary phenomenon, but would have shaped the way Roman observers perceived and understood the Germani even at first hand. People tend to see what they expect to see, and what people expected to see when they encountered Germani was what conventional wisdom about northern barbarians had led them to expect. Moreover, even apart from the pervasive influence of stereotypes, misperceptions and misinterpretations are inevitable when people from one culture try to observe and understand those from another. It is clear that, throughout *Germania*, Tacitus was interpreting Germanic institutions in terms of familiar Roman ones and no doubt distorting them, deliberately or not, in the process.

Another problem affects the second part of *Germania* in particular. Both Tacitus and his sources seem to have worked primarily not with maps, which plotted the location of peoples in relation to two-dimensional space, but rather with itineraries or descriptions of trade routes, which located peoples in relation either to some major topographical feature (e.g., along the Rhine) or, more commonly, to each other. Hence we find that Tacitus repeatedly locates a people 'beyond' or 'next to' or 'behind' another. In many cases it is impossible to determine what precise geographical location Tacitus actually had in mind, and we may suspect that in some cases he himself did not know. As a result, he was not always able to correlate information taken from different sources. Consequently, it would be rash to suppose that the second half of *Germania* contains anything like a comprehensive account of the Germanic peoples of Tacitus' day.

Some, perhaps much, of the information that Tacitus includes in *Germania* is thus unreliable. On the other hand, the labour of earlier scholars was not in vain; in some cases we can indeed corroborate Tacitus' observations with evidence from other sources. The real difficulty is that in the absence of such corroboration we simply cannot judge where Tacitus' account is reliable and where it is not. But as with *Agricola*, it is important to remember that Tacitus did not write *Germania* in order to provide us with the sorts of data that we would like to have, but rather as a literary exploration of themes and issues that concerned and interested him. It is thus above all as a work of literature that we should appreciate it.

NOTES

1. All dates subsequently are AD unless specified otherwise.

2. A. R. Birley, 'The Life and Death of Cornelius Tacitus', *Historia* 49.2 (2000), pp. 230–47.

3. *Orientis Graeci Inscriptiones Selectae*, ed. S. Dittenberger (Leipzig, 1903–5), no. 487.

4. A. R. Birley, *The Roman Government of Britain* (Oxford: Oxford University Press, 2005), pp. 77–8.

5. J. G. C. Anderson, ed., *Cornelii Taciti De Origine et Situ Germanorum* (Oxford: Clarendon Press, 1938; reprinted London: Bristol Classical Press, 1997), p. xxviii.

6. Ronald Syme, *Tacitus* (Oxford: Clarendon Press, 1958), pp. 127–8.

Further Reading

In my Introduction and notes I have frequently relied on the work of other scholars; more detailed discussions of the topics that I cover, along with guides to the extensive secondary literature, may be found in the following works.

Tacitus and His Writings

General

Ash, Rhiannon, *Tacitus* (London: Bristol Classical Press, 2006)

Birley, Anthony R., 'The Life and Death of Cornelius Tacitus', *Historia* 49.2 (2000), pp. 230–47

Martin, Ronald, *Tacitus* (Berkeley and Los Angeles: University of California Press, 1981)

Mellor, Ronald, *Tacitus* (London and New York: Routledge, 1993)

Shumate, Nancy, 'Tacitus and the Rhetoric of Empire', in her *Nation, Empire, Decline: Studies in Rhetorical Continuity from the Romans to the Modern Era* (London: Duckworth, 2006), pp. 81–127

Syme, Ronald, *Tacitus* (Oxford: Clarendon Press, 1958)

Agricola

Birley, Anthony R., *Tacitus:* Agricola *and* Germany; translated with an introduction and notes (Oxford: Oxford University Press, 1999)

Haynes, Holly, 'Survival and Memory in the *Agricola*', in Rhiannon Ash and Martha Malamud, eds., Ingens Eloquentiae

Materia: *Rhetoric and Empire in Tacitus* (= *Arethusa*, vol. 39.2, 2006), pp. 149–70

Ogilvie, R. M., and Ian Richmond, eds., *Cornelii Taciti De Vita Agricolae* (Oxford: Clarendon Press, 1967)

Germania

Anderson, J. G. C., ed., *Cornelii Taciti De Origine et Situ Germanorum* (Oxford: Clarendon Press, 1938; reprinted London: Bristol Classical Press, 1997)

Benario, Herbert, *Tacitus:* Germania; with an introduction, translation and commentary (Warminster: Aris & Phillips, 1999)

Rives, J. B., *Tacitus:* Germania; translated with an introduction and commentary (Oxford: Clarendon Press, 1999)

Historical Background
Iron Age Cultures in Northern Europe

Cunliffe, Barry, *Iron Age Communities in Britain* (4th edn, London and New York: Routledge, 2005)

Todd, Malcolm, *The Northern Barbarians, 100 BC–AD 300* (rev. edn, Oxford: Blackwell, 1987)

—, *The Early Germans* (2nd edn, Oxford: Blackwell, 2004)

Wells, Peter S., *Beyond Celts, Germans and Scythians: Archaeology and Identity in Iron Age Europe* (London: Duckworth, 2002)

Roman History

Boatwright, Mary T., Daniel J. Gargola and Richard J. A. Talbert, *A Brief History of the Romans* (Oxford: Oxford University Press, 2006)

Goodman, Martin, *A History of the Roman World, 44 BC–AD 180* (London and New York: Routledge, 1997)

Le Glay, Marcel, Jean-Louis Voisin and Yann Le Bohec, *A History of Rome* (3rd edn, Oxford: Blackwell, 2005)

Roman Britain

Birley, Anthony R., *The Roman Government of Britain* (Oxford: Oxford University Press, 2005)

Bowman, Alan K., *Life and Letters on the Roman Frontier: Vindolanda and its People* (London: British Museum Press, 1994)

Frere, Sheppard S., *Britannia: A History of Roman Britain* (3rd edn, London: Routledge & Kegan Paul, 1987)

Mattingly, David, *An Imperial Possession: Britain in the Roman Empire* (London: Allen Lane, 2006)

Millett, Martin, *The Romanization of Britain: An Essay in Archaeological Interpretation* (Cambridge: Cambridge University Press, 1990)

Richmond, Ian, *Roman Britain*, 3rd edn, rev. Malcolm Todd (London: Penguin, 1995)

Salway, Peter, *Roman Britain* (Oxford: Clarendon Press, 1981)

Todd, Malcolm, ed., *A Companion to Roman Britain* (Oxford: Blackwell, 2004)

Rome and Germany

Carroll, Maureen, *Romans, Celts and Germans: The German Provinces of Rome* (Stroud: Tempus, 2001)

Creighton, J. D., and J. R. A. Wilson, eds., *Roman Germany: Studies in Cultural Interaction* (Portsmouth, RI: Journal of Roman Archaeology Supplementary Series 32, 1999)

Roymans, Nico, *Ethnic Identity and Imperial Power: The Batavians in the Early Roman Empire* (Amsterdam: Amsterdam University Press, 2004)

Wells, C. M., *The German Policy of Augustus: An Examination of the Archaeological Evidence* (Oxford: Clarendon Press, 1972)

A Note on the Text and Translation

Harold Mattingly based his translation on the Oxford Classical Text of Henry Furneaux, revised by J. G. C. Anderson: *Cornelii Taciti Opera Minora* (Oxford: Clarendon Press, 1939). I have based my revision on the more recent Oxford Classical Text, with editions of *Agricola* by R. M. Ogilvie, corrected by M. Winterbottom, and of *Germania* by M. Winterbottom: *Cornelii Taciti Opera Minora* (Oxford: Clarendon Press, 1975). In some places I have deviated from the latter, often simply in order to provide a coherent translation; in the notes I have discussed all the more important of these deviations.

Mattingly's translation, which Penguin first published in 1948, was fresh and vivid, and often succeeded in giving some sense of the carefully wrought prose of the Latin original. S. A. Handford, who revised Mattingly's translation for Penguin in 1970, altered it by rendering in literal detail a number of nuances that in Latin are merely implied; he thereby in some ways made the translation more accurate, but in other ways less representative of the Latin original. In my own revision I have gone back to Mattingly's original translation, and have tried to retain and even augment the qualities for which it was admired. In a few places I have updated his phraseology; more often I have simply tried to sharpen the style, to give even more of a sense of what it is like to read these works in the original Latin. One point in particular requires comment: I have retained the Roman forms of the names of some peoples and places, writing 'Britanni' and 'Britannia', 'Germani' and 'Germania', instead of 'Britons' and 'Britain', 'Germans' and 'Germany'. This is a reminder that the peoples and places denoted by these

Roman names were not identical with those denoted by their English derivatives.

Agricola and *Germania* are normally cited by numbered divisions conventionally known as 'chapters'; these divisions are the work not of Tacitus himself, but of an early modern editor of the text.

AGRICOLA

1. Famous men have from time immemorial had their life stories told, and even our generation, with all its indifference to the present, has not quite abandoned the practice; outstanding personalities still win an occasional triumph over that fault common to small and great states alike, ignorant hostility to merit. But in the past, just as the road to memorable achievement was not so uphill or so beset with obstacles, so too the task of recording it never failed to attract men of genius. They wrote without currying favour or grinding their own axe, since the consciousness of an honourable aim was reward enough. Men even felt that to tell their own life's story showed self-confidence rather than conceit. Rutilius and Scaurus told theirs,[1] and were neither disbelieved nor criticized. It is true indeed that noble character is best appreciated in those ages in which it can most readily develop. But today, when I set out to recount the life of one no longer with us, I had to beg an indulgence[2] that I would not have sought for an invective: so savage and hostile to virtue are our times.

2. We have read that when eulogies were written – of Paetus Thrasea by Arulenus Rusticus and of Priscus Helvidius by Herennius Senecio[3] – they were treated as capital offences, and the savage punishment was extended beyond the authors to their very books: the *triumviri*[4] were given the job of burning those masterpieces of literary art in the Comitium and the Forum.[5] No doubt they believed that by that fire the voice of the Roman people, the freedom of the Senate and the moral consciousness of the human race were wiped out; even teachers of philosophy and all honourable studies were banished,[6] so that nothing

decent might be encountered anywhere. We have indeed left an impressive example of subservience. Just as Rome of old explored the limits of freedom, so have we plumbed the depths of slavery, robbed by informers even of the interchange of speech. We would have lost our memories as well as our tongues had it been as easy to forget as to be silent.

3. Now at long last our spirit revives. In the first dawn of this blessed age, Nerva Caesar harmonized the old discord of autocracy and freedom; day by day Nerva Trajan[7] is enhancing the happiness of the times; and the public security, ceasing to be merely something hoped and prayed for, is as solid and certain as a prayer fulfilled. Yet human nature is so weak that the cure lags behind the disease. As our bodies, which grow so slowly, perish in a flash, so too the mind and its interests can be more easily crushed than brought again to life. Idleness gradually becomes sweet, and we end by loving the sloth that at first we loathed. Moreover, in a period of fifteen years – no small part of a human life – many have died a natural death, and all the most irrepressible have fallen victim to the cruelty of the emperor.[8] Even we few who survive have outlived not only our fellows but also, so to speak, ourselves: so many years have been taken from our lives, years that have brought young men to old age, old men to the far end of life's journey – with no word said. Yet I shall find some satisfaction, even with unskilled and unpractised voice, in recording the servitude we once suffered and in gratefully acknowledging the blessings we now enjoy. In the meantime, this book, which sets out to honour my father-in-law Agricola, will be praised or at least pardoned for its profession of loyal affection.

4. Gnaeus Julius Agricola had his origins in the old and famous colony of Forum Julii.[9] Both his grandfathers were procurators of the Caesars – the equivalent of nobility in the equestrian order.[10] His father, Julius Graecinus, was a member of the Senate and won fame by his practice of eloquence and philosophy.[11] By those very accomplishments he incurred the wrath of Gaius Caesar; he received orders to accuse Marcus Silanus and lost his life for refusing.[12] His mother was Julia Procilla, a paragon of feminine virtue. Brought up under her tender care, he passed his boyhood and youth being trained in

all the liberal arts. He was shielded from the temptations of bad companions, partly by his own sound instincts, partly by living and going to school from his very early years at Massilia, a place where Greek refinement and provincial puritanism meet in a happy blend.[13] I remember how he would often tell us that in his early manhood he would have drunk deeper of philosophy than a Roman and a senator properly may, if his mother in her prudence had not damped the fire of his passion. It was only natural that such a fine and upright soul should be attracted strongly, if not too wisely, by the fair ideal of fame in its higher and nobler aspects. In time, the discretion that grows with age restrained him; he came away from philosophy with its hardest lesson learned – a sense of proportion.

5. He served his military apprenticeship in Britannia, to the satisfaction of Suetonius Paulinus,[14] that sound and thorough general, and was picked by him to be tried out on his staff. But Agricola was no loose young subaltern, to turn his military career into a debauch, nor did he make his tribuneship and inexperience an excuse for amusing himself and taking leaves. Instead, he got to know his province and be known by the army; he learned from the experts and followed the best models; he never sought a task for self-advertisement, never shirked one through cowardice. He was always energetic; careless, never.

Neither before nor since has Britannia ever been in a more uneasy or dangerous state: veterans butchered, colonies burned to the ground, armies isolated.[15] They had to fight for life before they could think of victory. The campaign was of course conducted under the strategy and leadership of another, and overall responsibility and the glory of recovering the province fell to the general. Yet everything combined to give the young Agricola fresh skill, fresh experience and fresh ambition, and his spirit was invaded by the passion for military glory – a thankless passion in an age when distinction was misconstrued and a great reputation was as dangerous as a bad one.

6. From Britannia Agricola returned to Rome to enter on his career of office, and married Domitia Decidiana, the child of an illustrious house.[16] It was a union that lent him both distinction and material aid to his ambitions. They lived in rare accord,

criticism of bonos mores

maintained by mutual affection and unselfishness, although in
such a partnership a good wife deserves more of the praise, just
as a bad one deserves more of the blame. In the draw for the
quaestorship he got Asia as his province and Salvius Titianus as
his proconsul[17] – and yet was corrupted by neither, although
the province with its wealth invited abuses, and the proconsul,
an abject slave to greed, was prepared to purchase by his ample
indulgence a mutual concealment of crimes. While in Asia he was
blessed with a daughter, and his position was thus strengthened
and his heart consoled for the loss of a son born not long before.

He passed the interval between quaestorship and tribuneship
of the people, and his actual year of office as tribune, in quiet
inactivity; he understood the age of Nero, in which an absence
of initiative proved good philosophy. His praetorship ran the
same quiet course, for no administration of law had fallen to
his lot. Over the games and other vanities of his office he com-
promised between economy and abundance, steering clear of
extravagance but not missing popular approval. He was then
chosen by Galba to check over the gifts in the temples, and by
his searching scrutiny achieved such a striking success that the
commonwealth seemed to perceive no sacrilege but Nero's.[18]

7. The following year dealt a grievous blow to his heart and
home. The men of Otho's fleet, while savagely plundering the territory of the Intimilians[19] in Liguria during their piratical career,
murdered Agricola's mother on her estate, and pillaged the estate
and a large part of her fortune, which was the motive for the murder. Agricola had accordingly set out to pay his last respects, when
he was overtaken by the news of Vespasian's bid for the empire,
and without a moment's hesitation joined his party. The initial
policy of the reign and the ordering of Rome were in the hands of
Mucianus,[20] since Domitian was still a young man and exploited
his father's success only to indulge himself. Mucianus sent Agricola to levy new troops and, when he had performed that task
with scrupulous zeal, put him in command of the Twentieth
Legion.[21] It had been slow to transfer its allegiance, and its commander was reported to be disloyal. As a matter of fact, the legion
was a problem and a menace even to consular legates, so naturally its legate, being merely of praetorian rank, was impotent to

large armies given to underprepared commanders

control it: perhaps he was to blame, perhaps his troops were. Agricola was thus chosen as both successor and avenger. But with a rare restraint he let it appear that he had found in his legion the loyalty he had created.

8. Britannia at that time was governed by Vettius Bolanus[22] with a hand too gentle for a warlike province. Agricola reined in his energies and restrained his enthusiasm, lest it grow too great; he was a master of tact, and had schooled himself to temper honour with expediency. Soon afterwards Britannia welcomed the consular Petilius Cerialis.[23] Agricola's worth now found scope for its display, but at first it was only hard work and danger that Cerialis shared – glory came later. Cerialis often divided the armies with him, to test his quality, and when he had stood the test sometimes put him in command of larger forces. Yet Agricola never bragged of his achievements; as a mere subordinate he credited every success to his inspirer and leader. Thus by his gallantry in action and by the modesty of his reports he evaded envy without missing renown.

9. On Agricola's return to Rome from the command of the legion, Divus Vespasian enrolled him among the patricians and then placed him in command of the province of Aquitania.[24] It was a brilliant promotion to a post important in itself and implying expectation of the consulship, for which Agricola was in fact marked out. It is a common belief that military men lack subtlety of temperament, and indeed martial law, knowing no appeal and proceeding bluntly to its usually summary decisions, gives no scope to the craftiness of the law courts. But Agricola, although dealing with civilians, had enough good sense to be natural and just. He made a clear division between hours of business and relaxation. When legal cases demanded attention, he was dignified and serious, strict yet inclined to mercy. When duty had had its due, he put off the official pose; harshness, arrogance and greed had long ceased to be part of his make-up. He succeeded where few succeed: he lost no authority by his affability, but no affection by his sternness. To mention incorruptibility and self-restraint in a man of his calibre would be to insult his virtues. Although the desire for fame is often a secret weakness even of the good, Agricola never courted it by advertisement or

intrigue. Scorning all rivalry with his colleagues, all bickering
with the procurators, he deemed it no triumph to override others,
but ignominious to be overborne himself.

He was kept in this command for less than three years and
then called home to the immediate prospect of the consulship.
Public opinion insisted that the province of Britannia was
intended for him, not because he himself said anything about it,
but because he was obviously the right man. Rumour does not
always err; it may even prompt a selection. In his consulship he
betrothed to me, in my early manhood, his daughter, a girl of
rare promise, and after its close gave her to me in marriage.
Immediately afterwards he received the command of Britannia,
together with the priestly office of pontifex.

10. Though the position and peoples of Britannia[25] have been
described by many writers, I am going to describe them again,
not to match my industry and ability against theirs, but because
only at that time was the conquest completed: where my predecessors adorned their guesses with grace of style, I shall offer
assured fact.

Britannia, the largest of the islands known to us Romans, is
so shaped and situated as to face Germania, on the east and
Hispania on the west,[26] while to the south it can actually be seen
by the Gauls. Its northern shores, with no lands facing them, are
beaten by a wild and open sea. Livy and Fabius Rusticus[27] – the
most articulate of older and more recent writers respectively –
compared the shape of Britannia as a whole to an elongated
diamond or a double-bladed axe.[28] Such indeed is its shape this
side of Caledonia, and has consequently been attributed to the
whole. But when you have crossed over, a huge and shapeless
tract of country juts out from what had seemed to be the land's
end and tapers into a kind of wedge. The coast of this remotest
sea was at that time first rounded by a Roman fleet, thus proving that Britannia was an island.[29] It also discovered and subdued hitherto unknown islands called the Orcades.[30] Thule,[31]
too, was sighted by our men, but no more; their orders took
them no farther, and winter was close at hand.

But they report that the sea is sluggish and heavy to the oar
and, even with the wind, does not rise as other seas do.[32] The

reason, I think, is that lands and mountains, which create and
sustain storms, are scarcer there, and the deep mass of an unbroken sea is more slowly set in motion. To investigate the nature
of the Ocean and its tides lies outside my immediate scope, and
the matter has been much discussed. I will add just one point:
nowhere does the sea hold wider sway. It carries to and fro a
mass of currents, and in its ebb and flow is not restricted to the
coast, but passes deep inland and winds about, pushing in even
among highlands and mountains as if in its own domain.

11. Who the first inhabitants of Britannia were, whether
natives or immigrants, remains obscure, as one would expect
when dealing with barbarians. But their physical characteristics
vary, and that variation is suggestive. The reddish hair and large
limbs of the Caledonians proclaim a Germanic origin;[33] the
swarthy faces of the Silures, their generally curly hair and the
fact that Hispania lies opposite, all lead one to believe that
Iberians crossed in ancient times and occupied that land. Those
nearest the Gauls are also like them. Perhaps their common
origin still has force, perhaps their common situation under the
heavens[34] has shaped the physical type in lands that extend in
different directions.

On a general estimate, however, it is likely that Gauls took
possession of the neighbouring island. In both lands you find
the same rituals, the same superstitious beliefs; the language
does not differ much; there is the same boldness in courting
danger and, when it has come, the same cowardice in avoiding
it.[35] Yet the Britanni show more spirit; they have not yet been
softened by protracted peace. The Gauls, too, we are told, were
once pre-eminent in war; but then with peace came sloth, and
valour was lost with liberty. The same thing has happened to
those of the Britanni who have long been conquered; the rest
are still as the Gauls once were.[36]

12. Their strength is in their infantry. Some tribes also fight
with chariots.[37] The nobleman drives, his dependants fight in
his defence. At one time they owed obedience to kings; now
they are divided into factions and groups under rival leaders.
Indeed, nothing has helped us more in war with their strongest
nations than their inability to cooperate.[38] It is but seldom that

tribalism / fractured peoples

two or three states unite to repel a common danger; fighting separately, they are conquered all together.

The climate is foul with frequent rains and mists, but there is no extreme cold. Their day is longer than in our part of the world. The night is bright and, in the furthest part of Britannia, so short that you can barely distinguish the evening from the morning twilight. If no clouds block the view, the sun's glow, they say, can be seen all night long: it does not set and rise, but simply passes along the horizon. In fact, the flat ends of the earth cannot, with their low shadow, raise the darkness to any height; night therefore fails to reach the sky and its stars.[39] *haha!*

The soil is productive of crops, except for olives, grapes and other natives of warmer climes, and rich in cattle. Crops are slow to ripen, but quick to grow – both facts due to one and the same cause, the abundant moisture of land and sky. Britannia yields gold, silver and other metals, a reward for victory. The Ocean, too, produces pearls, but they are dusky and mottled. Some think that those who gather them lack skill. Whereas in the Red Sea[40] they are torn alive and breathing from the rocks, in Britannia they are collected as the sea throws them up. I find more plausible a lack of quality in pearls than of greed in us.

13. The Britanni themselves readily submit to the levy, the tribute and the other obligations of empire, provided that there is no abuse. That they bitterly resent, for they have been broken in to obedience, not to slavery. Divus Julius, the first Roman to enter Britannia with an army, did indeed intimidate the natives by a victory and gain control of the coast, but he can be said to have pointed it out, not handed it over, to posterity.[41] Then came the civil wars, with the weapons of Roman leaders turned against the commonwealth. But even in peace, Britannia was long out of mind. Divus Augustus called this 'policy', Tiberius 'precedent'.[42] Gaius Caesar unquestionably planned an invasion of Britannia, but his quick fancies shifted like a weathervane, and his vast efforts against Germania came to naught.[43] It was Divus Claudius who was responsible for the great undertaking: he sent over legions and auxiliaries and chose Vespasian as his colleague[44] – the first step towards his future greatness. Nations were subdued, kings were captured and Vespasian was marked out by fate.

(margin notes: Unmarked bias & feeling of superiority)

(margin notes: & condition of enfranchise joining Roman umbrella)

(margin notes: & all emperors deified)

(margin notes: Caesar venerated → De Bello Gall. 5:6)

14. Aulus Plautius[45] was the first consular to be appointed governor, and soon after him came Ostorius Scapula[46] – both men with distinguished military records. The nearest parts of Britannia were gradually shaped into a province, and moreover a colony of veterans was founded.[47] Certain states were presented to King Togidumnus,[48] who maintained his unswerving loyalty down to our own times – an example of the long-established Roman custom of employing even kings to make others slaves. Didius Gallus,[49] the next governor, held on to what his predecessors had won, and even pushed a few forts into more advanced positions, so that he could boast of having extended his sphere of duty. Veranius[50] succeeded Didius, only to die within the year. After him, Suetonius Paulinus[51] enjoyed two years of success, conquering tribes and strengthening garrisons. Emboldened thereby to attack the island of Mona, on the grounds that it was feeding native resistance, he exposed himself to attack in the rear.

15. For the Britanni, freed from fear by the absence of the legate, began to discuss the woes of slavery, to compare their wrongs and sharpen their sting in the telling.[52] 'We gain nothing by submission except heavier burdens for shoulders shown to be willing. Once we had one king at a time, now two are clamped on us – the legate to wreak his fury on our lives, the procurator on our property. We subjects are damned in either case, whether our masters quarrel or agree. Their gangs, the centurions of the one and the slaves of the other, mingle violence and insult. Nothing now is safe from their greed, nothing safe from their lust. In battle it is the braver who takes the spoil; as things stand with us, it is mostly cowards and shirkers who rob our homes, kidnap our children and conscript our men, as though it were only for our country that we know not how to die. But what a mere handful our invaders are, if we Britanni reckon up our own numbers! The Germani, reckoning so, threw off the yoke,[53] and they had only a river, not the Ocean, to shield them. We have country, wives and parents to fight for; the Romans have only greed and self-indulgence. They will withdraw, as Divus Julius withdrew, if only we can rival the valour of our fathers. We must not panic at the loss of a

battle or two; success may foster a boldness in attack, but suffering gives power to endure. The gods themselves at last show mercy to us Britanni, by keeping the Roman general away and his army exiled in another island. For ourselves, we have already taken the most difficult step – we have begun to plan. And in undertakings like this it is more dangerous to be caught planning than to take the plunge.'

16. Goaded by such mutual encouragements, the whole island rose in arms under the command of Boudicca,[54] a woman of royal descent – for Britanni make no distinction of sex in the appointment of leaders.[55] They hunted down the Roman troops in their scattered posts, stormed the forts and assaulted the colony itself,[56] which they saw as the seat of their enslavement; nor did the angry victors deny themselves any of the savagery characteristic of barbarians. In fact, had not Paulinus, on hearing of the revolt, hurriedly come to help, Britannia would have been lost. As it was, he restored it to its old obedience by a single successful action. But many rebels refused to lay down arms, conscious of their guilt and having a special dread of the legate. Fine officer though he was, they feared that he would abuse their surrender and punish with undue severity wrongs that he viewed as personal.

Petronius Turpilianus[57] was thus sent out in his place, as someone more merciful and readier to forgive offences to which he was a stranger. He pacified the previous troubles, but risked no further move before handing over his province to Trebellius Maximus.[58] Trebellius, a bit lazy and lacking military experience, maintained his province by an affable administration. The barbarians now learned like us to condone seductive vices, while the intervention of the civil wars gave a reasonable excuse for inactivity. There was, however, some serious trouble with mutiny, for the troops, accustomed to campaigns, ran riot in peace. Trebellius fled and hid to escape his angry army. Dishonoured and despised, he soon returned to command on sufferance; by a kind of tacit bargain the troops retained their licence, the general his life, and the mutiny stopped short of bloodshed. Vettius Bolanus,[59] likewise, as the civil wars still ran their course, declined to disturb Britannia by enforcing discipline. There was the same lack of

action in face of the foe, the same indiscipline in the camp – only
Bolanus was a decent man, with no misdeeds to make him hated,
and had won affection where he lacked authority.

17. But when Vespasian recovered Britannia, together with the
rest of the world, the generals were great, the armies outstanding
and the hopes of our enemies diminished. Petilius Cerialis[60] at
once struck terror into their hearts by attacking the state of the
Brigantes, said to be the most populous in the whole province.
After a series of battles, some not uncostly, he had conquered or
at least overrun a great part of their territory.[61] Cerialis, indeed,
would have eclipsed the record and reputation of any ordinary
successor. But Julius Frontinus[62] took up and shouldered the
heavy burden, as great a man as the times allowed. He subdued
by force of arms the strong and warlike nation of the Silures,
triumphing over a difficult terrain as well as a brave enemy.

18. Such was the state of Britannia, such the vicissitudes of
war that Agricola found when he crossed the channel with the
summer half over, at a season when, with campaigning presumably done for the year, our troops pursue their rest and our enemies
their opportunity. Shortly before his arrival the state of the
Ordovices had almost wiped out a squadron of cavalry stationed
in their territory, and this initial stroke had excited the province.
Those who wished for war welcomed the lead, and waited only
to test the temper of the new legate. The summer was far spent,
the auxiliaries were scattered over the province, the legionaries
took it for granted that there would be no more fighting that
year. Everything, in fact, combined to hamper or thwart a new
campaign, and many were in favour of simply watching where
the danger lay. Even so, Agricola decided to go and meet the
threat. He drew together detachments of the legions and a small
force of auxiliaries. As the Ordovices did not venture to meet
him in the plain, he marched his men into the hills, with himself
in the front of the line to lend his own courage to the rest by
sharing their peril, and slaughtered almost the entire nation.

He realized, however, that he must follow up on this advantage, and that the outcome of his first operations would determine the level of terror that the others would inspire. He decided,
therefore, to reduce the island of Mona, from the occupation of

which Paulinus had been recalled by the revolt of all Britannia, as I described above. But as often happens when plans are hastily conceived, he had no ships; it was the resource and resolution of the general that took the troops across. Agricola carefully picked out from his auxiliaries those who were familiar with the fords and had a tradition of swimming with arms and horses under control,[63] and made them discard all their equipment. He then sent them in so suddenly that the enemy, who had been thinking in terms of fleet, ships and naval warfare, completely lost their heads: what could delay or defeat a foe who attacked like that? They sued for peace and surrendered the island, and Agricola won great reputation and respect. Had he not, on his very first entrance to the province, a time usually devoted to pageantry and ceremonial visits, deliberately chosen a difficult and dangerous enterprise? Yet Agricola did not let success tickle his vanity. He had kept in check a conquered people; he would not call that a campaign of conquest. He did not even use laurel-wreathed dispatches to announce his achievement. But his very refusal to acknowledge his fame increased it: what hopes he must have for the future when he could afford to ignore such great deeds as these!

19. Agricola, however, understood the feelings of a province and had learned from the experience of others that arms effect little if injustice follows behind. And so he resolved to root out the causes of war. Beginning with himself and his staff, he enforced discipline in his own household first – a task that many find as difficult as governing a province. He made no use of freedmen or slaves for public business. He was not influenced by personal feelings or by recommendations or petitions in choosing centurions and soldiers for his staff, but thought that the best would best justify his trust. He knew everything, but did not always act as if he knew. Minor offences he overlooked, but he had no mercy for major ones. Yet he did not always punish; more often than not he was content with repentance. He preferred to appoint to official positions and duties men who would not transgress, rather than punish them when they did.

He eased the levy of grain and tribute by distributing the burden fairly, and put an end to the tricks of profiteers that were more

[handwritten marginalia: How different is being a Roman territory to creating a federal soul]

bitterly resented than the tax itself.[64] The provincials had actually been compelled to wait at the doors of closed granaries, in order, moreover, to buy grain and so discharge their duty by payment. Roundabout routes and distant destinations were stipulated, so that states that had permanent camps close by had to send to remote and inaccessible spots. In the end, what should have been easy for all became profitable for a few. 20. By checking these abuses in his very first year of office, Agricola gave men reason to love and honour peace, which, through the negligence or arrogance of former governors, had been as much feared as war.

But when summer came and he had brought together his army, he was present everywhere on the march, praising discipline and checking stragglers. He himself chose the sites for camps, he himself reconnoitred estuaries and woods, and all the time he gave the enemy no rest, but constantly launched plundering raids. Then, when he had done enough to inspire fear, he turned to mercy and offered the allurements of peace. As a result, many states that had till then maintained their independence laid aside their resentment, gave hostages and accepted the curb of garrisons and forts.[65] So skilfully and thoroughly was the whole operation carried through that no new part of Britannia was ever acquired with so few problems.

21. The following winter was spent on measures of the most salutary kind. To induce a people, hitherto scattered, uncivilized and therefore prone to fight, to grow pleasurably inured to peace and ease, Agricola encouraged individuals and assisted communities to build temples, public squares and proper houses.[66] He praised the keen and scolded the slack, and competition for honour worked as well as compulsion. Furthermore, he trained the sons of the leading men in the liberal arts[67] and preferred the natural ability of the Britanni over the trained skill of the Gauls. The result was that in place of distaste for the Latin language came a passion to command it.[68] In the same way, our national dress came into favour and the toga was everywhere to be seen. And so they strayed into the enticements of vice – porticoes, baths and sumptuous banquets. In their innocence they called this 'civilization', when in fact it was a part of their enslavement.

[handwritten marginalia: Civilising mission / condescension; Praise language]

22. The third year of campaigning opened up new nations, for the territory of tribes as far as the estuary named the Taus was ravaged.[69] Although our army was severely buffeted by furious storms, the enemy were now too terrified to molest it. There was even time to spare for constructing forts. It is observed by experts that no general has ever shown a better eye for suitable sites than Agricola. No fort of his was ever stormed or ever abandoned through surrender or flight. In fact, the men made frequent sallies, for they were protected against long siege by supplies to last a year. Thus winter in these forts was free from fear, and each could take care of itself. The enemy were baffled and near despair; they had been used to making good the losses of the summer by the gains of the winter, but were now hard pressed in both seasons alike.

Agricola was never greedy in stealing the credit for other men's work. Every centurion and prefect found in him an honest witness to his merit. By some accounts, he could be very bitter in reprimand, and certainly he was as nasty to the wrong kind of man as he was nice to the right. But no secret resentment remained from his anger, so that you had no need to fear his silence. He thought it more honourable to hurt than to hate.

23. The fourth summer was spent in securing the districts already overrun, and, if the valour of our armies and the glory of Rome had not forbidden a halt, a place for halting would have been found within Britannia itself.[70] For the Clota and Bodotria, carried far back inland by the tides of opposite seas, are separated by only a narrow neck of land. This neck was now secured by garrisons, and the whole sweep of land to the south was safe in our hands. The enemy were pushed into what was virtually another island.

24. In the fifth year of campaigning Agricola journeyed by sea on the lead ship, and in a series of successful actions subdued nations hitherto unknown.[71] The whole side of Britannia that faces Hibernia was lined with his forces, with hope rather than fear as his motive. Hibernia, lying between Britannia and Hispania[72] and easily accessible also from the Gallic Sea, might to great general advantage bind more closely that powerful part of the empire. In extent Hibernia is smaller than Britannia, but

larger than the islands of our sea. In soil, in climate and in *The*
the character and civilization of its <u>inhabitants it is much like</u> *Éire*
<u>Britannia</u>. Its approaches and harbours are tolerably well known *are*
from merchants who trade there. Agricola had welcomed an *also*
Hibernian prince, who had been driven from home by rebellion; *celtic*
nominally a friend, he might be used as a pawn in the game.
I often heard Agricola say that Hibernia could be reduced and
held by a single legion and a few auxiliaries, and that the conquest would also pay with regard to Britannia, if Roman arms
were in evidence on every side and liberty vanished off the map.

25. In the summer with which his sixth year of office began,
Agricola enveloped the states that lie beyond the Bodotria.[73]
Fearing a general rising of the peoples beyond and routes endan-
gered by a hostile army, he used his fleet to reconnoitre the harbours. This was initially used by Agricola to bring his forces up
to strength, but its continued attendance made an excellent
impression. For the war was pushed forward simultaneously by
land and sea, and often in the same camp infantry and cavalry on
the one hand and marines on the other would share rations and
exuberance. Each side boasted, as soldiers will, of its own exploits
and adventures, and matched the perilous depths of woods and
mountains against the hazards of storms and tides, the victories
over enemies on land against the conquest of the Ocean. The
Britanni, for their part, as was learned from prisoners, were
stupefied by the appearance of the fleet, as though the mystery
of their sea was divulged and their last refuge in defeat cut off.

The natives of <u>Caledonia turned to armed resistance on a
grand scale, even grander, as is usual with the unknown, in</u> report.
They went so far as to attack our forts, and inspired alarm by
taking the offensive. Cowards in the council, pretending prudence, pleaded for a 'strategic retreat' behind the Bodotria and
claimed that 'evacuation is preferable to expulsion'. But just then
Agricola learned that the enemy were about to attack in several
columns. To avoid encirclement by superior forces familiar with
the territory, he likewise divided his own army into three parts
and so advanced.

26. As soon as the enemy got to know of this they suddenly
changed their plans and massed for a night attack on the Ninth

Legion, which seemed to them the weakest. Striking panic into the sleeping camp, they cut down the sentries and broke in. The fight was already raging inside the camp when Agricola was warned by his scouts of the enemy's march. Following closely on their tracks, he ordered the speediest of his cavalry and infantry to harass the assailants' rear and then had his whole army join in the battle cry; the standards gleamed in the light of dawn. The Britanni were dismayed at being caught between two fires, while the men of the Ninth took heart again; with their lives now safe they could fight for honour. They even effected a sally, and a grim struggle ensued in the narrow passage of the gates. At last the enemy broke under the rival efforts of the two armies – the one striving to make it plain that they had brought relief, the other that they could have done without it. Had not marshes and woods covered the enemy's retreat, that victory would have ended the war.

27. Fired with self-confidence and the glory of this victory, the army clamoured that nothing could bar its brave advance: 'we must drive deeper and deeper into Caledonia and fight battle after battle till we have reached the end of Britannia.' Even those who had just been so cautious and wise were brave and boastful after the fact. This is the crowning injustice of war; all claim credit for success, while defeat is laid to the account of one. The Britanni, on their side, felt that they had not lost through any lack of courage, but through chance exploited by the general's skill. With unbroken spirit they persisted in arming their youth, putting their wives and children in places of safety and ratifying their league by conference and sacrifice. The campaign thus ended with tempers on both sides raised to fever-pitch.

28. That same summer a cohort of Usipi[74] that had been levied in Germania and transferred to Britannia committed a crime remarkable enough to deserve record.[75] They murdered the centurion and soldiers who had been mingled in their ranks to teach them discipline and serve as models and directors, then boarded three Liburnians,[76] constraining the pilots to do their will. Two of these incurred suspicion and were put to death, the third was set to rowing. As their story was still unknown, they sailed along the coasts like an apparition. When they put into

land to get water and other necessities, they came to blows with the Britanni, who defended their property; often successful, they were sometimes repulsed. They were finally reduced to such straits of famine that they first ate the weakest of their number and then victims drawn by lot. And thus they sailed right round Britannia. Having lost their ships through bad seamanship, they were taken for pirates and cut off first by the Suebi and then by the Frisii.[77] Some of them were sold as slaves and passed from hand to hand till they reached our bank of the Rhine, where they gained notoriety from the tale of their great adventure.

29. At the beginning of the next summer Agricola suffered a grievous personal loss in the death of the son who had been born the year before.[78] This cruel blow drew from him neither the ostentatious stoicism of the strong man nor the loud expressions of grief that belong to women. The conduct of war was one of the means he had to relieve his sorrow. He sent his fleet ahead to plunder at various points and thus spread uncertainty and terror; then, with his army marching light, having reinforced it with the bravest of the Britanni whose loyalty had been proved during a long peace, he reached Mons Graupius.[79] It was already occupied by the enemy. The Britanni were, in fact, undaunted by the loss of the previous battle, and awaited either revenge or enslavement. They had realized at last that the common danger must be met by common action, and had sent round embassies and drawn up treaties to rally the full force of all their states. Already more than 30,000 men could be seen, and still they came – all the young men and those whose 'old age was fresh and green',[80] famous warriors wearing their marks of martial glory.

At that point one of the many leaders, named Calgacus,[81] a man outstanding in valour and family, spoke before the assembled masses of men demanding battle, in words, we are told, like these. 30. 'Whenever I consider why we are fighting and how we have reached this crisis, I have a strong sense that this day of your splendid rally will be the dawn of freedom for the whole of Britannia. You have mustered to a man, and to a man you are free. There are no lands behind us, and even the sea is menaced by the Roman fleet. The clash of battle – the hero's

glory – has become the coward's safest refuge. Earlier battles
against the Romans were won or lost, but never without hope:
we were always there in reserve. We, the choice flower of Britannia, have been treasured in her most secret places. Out of
sight of subject shores, even our eyes are free from the defile-
ment of tyranny. We, the last men of the earth and the last of
the free, have been shielded till today by the very remoteness of
our rumoured land. But now the boundary of Britannia is
exposed, and everything unknown is valued all the more.
Beyond us lies no other nation, nothing but waves and rocks
and Romans, more deadly still than they, whose arrogance no
submission or moderation can elude. Brigands of the world,
after exhausting the land by their wholesale plunder they now
ransack the sea. The wealth of an enemy excites their greed, his
poverty their lust for power. Neither East nor West has served
to glut their maw. Only they, of all on earth, long for the poor
with as keen a desire as they do the rich. Robbery, butchery,
rapine, these the liars call "empire": they create desolation and
call it peace.

31. 'Our children and kinsmen, by nature's law, we love
above all else. These are torn from us by conscription to slave
in other lands. Our wives and sisters, even if they are not raped
by Roman enemies, are seduced by them in the guise of guests
and friends. Our goods and fortunes are ground down to pay
tribute, our land and harvests to supply grain, our bodies and
hands to build roads through woods and swamps – all under
blows and insults. Slaves who are born into slavery are sold
only once, and are moreover maintained by their masters:
Britannia daily buys her own enslavement, daily feeds her
enslavers. And just as in a private household the latest arrival
is always abused by even his fellow slaves, so in this slave-
household of the world, as the Romans have long ago made it,
we are the cheap new acquisitions, picked out for extirpation;
we have no fertile lands, no mines, no harbours, which we
might be spared to work. Courage and martial spirit we have,
but these are qualities that rulers do not prize in their subjects.
Even our remoteness and seclusion, just as they protect, so
they also expose us to suspicion.

[margin left: Such a long reproach of Rome, recorded. What could be all the authors' motives for this?]

[margin right: Jealousy over male desire interesting psychological question of feelings of ownership over "their" women.]

'Abandon, then, all hope of mercy and at last take courage, whether it is life or honour that you hold most dear. The Brigantes,[82] with only a woman to lead them, burned a colony, stormed a camp and, if success had not made them careless, might have cast off the yoke. But we, uncorrupted and unconquered, are fighting to retain our freedom, not regain it after second thoughts;[83] let us prove at the first clash of arms what kind of men Caledonia has held in reserve. 32. Can you really imagine that the Romans' bravery in war measures up to their licence in peace? No! It is our quarrels and disunion that have given them fame; the reputation of the Roman army is built upon the faults of its enemies. Look at it, a motley agglomeration of nations,[84] that will be shattered by defeat as surely as it is now held together by success! Or can you seriously think that those Gauls and Germani – and, to our bitter shame, many Britanni too! – are bound to Rome by genuine loyalty or love? They may be lending their life-blood to foreign tyrants, but they were enemies of Rome much longer than they have been her slaves. Apprehension and terror are weak bonds of affection; just break them, and, where fear has ended, hatred will begin.

'All that can goad men to victory is on our side. The enemy have no wives to fire their courage, no parents ready to taunt them if they run away. Most of them have no homeland, or have one other than Rome. See them, a scanty band, scared and bewildered, staring blankly at the unfamiliar sky, sea and forests around! The gods have given them, like spellbound prisoners, into your hands. Have no fear for the empty pomp, the glitter of gold and silver that can neither avert nor inflict a wound. In the very ranks of our enemies we shall find hands to help us. The Britanni will recognize our cause as their own, the Gauls will recall their lost liberty, the rest of the Germani will desert them just as the Usipi have recently done. They have nothing in reserve that need alarm us – forts without garrisons, colonies of old men, towns sick and distracted between rebel subjects and tyrant masters. On this side you have a general and an army; on that, the tribute, the mines and the other penalties imposed on slaves. Whether you are to endure these for ever or take quick vengeance, this field must decide. On, then, into action and, as you go, think of those that went before you and of those that shall come after.' 33. This speech was received with enthusiasm, expressed, as barbarians do, in roars and songs and inarticulate shouts. Bodies of troops began to move and arms blazed, as the most adventurous ran out in front, and all the time their battle-line was taking shape.

Agricola's soldiers were in good heart and fretting at confinement within their defences. For all that, he thought it best to put the final edge on their courage and addressed them thus.[85] 'This is the seventh year, comrades, that by the valour and blessings of Rome and by our own loyal efforts you have been conquering Britannia. In all these campaigns, all these battles, which have required courage in face of the enemy and patient toil in face of Nature herself, I have had no complaint of my men nor you of your general. And so we have surpassed the limits of former legates and former armies. We grasp the farthest regions of Britannia, not by report or rumour, but by encamping here in force. Britannia has been explored and at the same time subdued. How often on the march, when you were making your weary way over marshes, mountains and rivers, have I heard the bravest of you exclaim, "When shall we find the enemy? When shall we come to grips?"[86] Now they come, dislodged from their lairs. The field lies open for valour, as you so bravely prayed. An easy path awaits you if you win, but a hard and uphill one if you lose. The miles of hard marching behind you, the woods you have threaded, the estuaries crossed – all redound to your credit and honour, as long as you keep your eyes to the front; if we retreat, however, our success in surmounting these obstacles will place us in deadliest peril. We lack the local knowledge of our enemy, we lack their abundant supplies; yet we have our hands and our swords, and with these we have all we need. For myself, I made up my mind long ago that no army and no general can safely turn their back. It follows, then, not only that a death of honour is better than a life of shame, but also that safety and renown are to be sought in the same field. And, if we must perish, it would be no mean glory to fall where land and nature end.

34. 'If you were confronted by strange nations and an unfamiliar army, I would cite the example of other armies to encourage you. As it is, you need only recall your own battle-honours, only question your own eyes. These are the men who just last year attacked a single legion like thieves in the night, only to be broken by your mere battle-cry. These are the Britanni with the longest legs – the only reason they have survived so long. When we would plunge into woods and thickets, all the brave beasts charged straight at us, while the timid and passive slunk away at the very sound of our march. It is just the same now: the best Britanni have fallen long since, and what remains is a pack of cowards and cravens. To be sure, at last you meet them face to face, but not because they have taken a stand: they have instead been caught. It is only extreme danger and deadly fear that have rooted them to this spot, where you may gain a brilliant and beautiful victory. Have done with campaigning, crown fifty years with one glorious day, convince the commonwealth that, if wars have dragged on or rebellions arisen, her soldiers have not been to blame!'

35. Even while Agricola was still speaking the troops showed visible signs of their keenness, and a wild burst of enthusiasm greeted the end of his speech. Without delay they flew to their arms. The troops were mad for action and ready to rush into it, but Agricola marshalled them with care. The auxiliary infantry, 8,000 in number, made a strong centre, while 3,000 cavalry were spread out on the flanks. The legions were stationed in front of the camp wall; victory would be vastly more glorious if it cost no Roman blood, whereas in case of repulse the legions could restore the day. The Britannic army was stationed on higher ground in order to impress and intimidate its enemy. Its front line was on level ground, but the other ranks were packed on a rising slope as though in tiers. The space between the two armies was filled by the charioteers,[87] clattering on in their wild career. At this point, Agricola, fearing that the enemy with their great superiority in numbers might fall simultaneously on his front and flanks, opened out his ranks. The line now looked dangerously thin, and many urged him to bring up the legions. But he, always an optimist and resolute amidst adversity, sent away his horse and took up his position on foot in front of the standards.

36. The fighting began with exchanges of missiles, and the Britanni showed both courage and skill in parrying our shots with their great swords or catching them on their little shields, while they in turn rained huge volleys on us. At last Agricola urged the four cohorts of Batavi and the two of Tungri[88] to move in and fight it out at the sword's point. The manoeuvre was familiar to those old soldiers, but awkward for the enemy with their small shields and unwieldy swords – for the swords of the Britanni lack a thrusting point, and so are unsuited to the clash of arms in close combat. The Batavi, striking blow after blow, pushing with the bosses of their shields and stabbing at their enemies' faces, routed the men on the plain and began to push the battle uphill. This provoked the rest of our cohorts to drive in hard and butcher the enemy as they met them. Many Britanni were left behind half dead or even unwounded, owing to the very speed of our victory. Our cavalry squadrons, meanwhile, had routed the war-chariots, and now plunged into the infantry battle. Their first onslaught was terrifying, but the solid ranks of the enemy and the roughness of the ground soon brought them to a standstill. The battle looked nothing like a cavalry action, with our men precariously perched on the slope and jostled by the flanks of the horses. And often stray chariots or riderless horses, careering about wildly in their terror, came plunging in on the ranks from flank or front.

37. The Britanni on the hill-tops had so far taken no part in the action, and had leisure to note with contempt the smallness of our numbers. They now began to make a slow descent and envelop our victorious rear. But Agricola, anticipating just such a move, threw in their path four squadrons of cavalry, which he was keeping in hand for emergencies. He thus broke and scattered them in a rout as severe as their assault had been fierce. The tactics of the Britanni were now turned against themselves. On the orders of their general, our squadrons rode round from the front and fell upon the enemy in the rear. The spectacle that followed over the open country was awe-inspiring and grim. Our men kept pursuing and wounding, capturing some and then killing them as others appeared. On the enemy's side each man now followed his bent. Some bands, though armed, fled before inferior

numbers; some men, though unarmed, deliberately charged to their deaths. Everywhere were weapons, bodies, mangled limbs and soil soaked with blood, and even the vanquished now and then found their fury and their courage again. For when they reached the woods, they rallied and profited by their local knowledge to ambush the first rash pursuers. Our excess of confidence might have led to disaster, but Agricola was everywhere at once. He ordered strong cohorts of lightly armed troops to ring the woods like hunters; where the woods were denser, he sent in dismounted cavalry to scour them, and where they thinned out, the cavalry did the work. But the Britanni, when they saw that our ranks were re-formed and steady and beginning the pursuit again, simply turned and ran. They no longer kept formation or looked to see where their comrades were, but scattered and, avoiding each other, made for distant and trackless retreats. Only night and exhaustion ended the pursuit. Of the enemy some 10,000 fell, on our side 360, among whom was Aulus Atticus, the prefect of a cohort, whose youthful enthusiasm and mettlesome horse took him deep into the ranks of the enemy.

38. That night, naturally, the victors rejoiced in their glory and booty. The Britanni dispersed, men and women wailing together, carrying off their wounded and calling out to the survivors. They abandoned their homes and in fury set fire to them; they chose hiding-places, only to abandon them at once. At times they met to form some sort of common plan, but then split up. Sometimes the sight of their dear ones broke their hearts, more often it enraged them; some, it was well known, laid violent hands on their wives and children as if in pity. The next day revealed more clearly the effects of the victory. An awful silence reigned on every hand, the hills were deserted, houses were smoking in the distance, and our scouts encountered no one. These, sent out in all directions, observed the random tracks of the fugitives and determined that the enemy were not massing at any point. Since summer was almost over and operations could not be extended more widely, Agricola led his army into the territory of the Boresti.[89] There he took hostages and ordered the prefect of the fleet to sail around Britannia. Sufficient forces were allotted, and the terror of Rome had gone before him.

Agricola himself, marching slowly in order to inspire fear in new nations by his very lack of hurry, placed his infantry and cavalry in winter quarters. At the same time, the fleet, sped by favouring winds and fame, reached the port of Trucculum,[90] from which it had set out to coast the neighbouring stretch of Britannia.

39. The news of these events, although reported by Agricola in his dispatches in the most exact and modest terms, was received by Domitian, as was his wont, with a smile on his face and unease in his heart. He was aware that his sham triumph over Germania[91] had been treated as a joke – slaves had been bought in the markets whose dress and hair were contrived to make them look like prisoners of war. But here was a genuine victory on a grand scale: the enemy dead were reckoned by thousands, the popular enthusiasm immense. There was nothing Domitian feared so much as to have the name of a subject raised above that of the prince. In vain had he silenced the eloquence of the courts and the distinctions of civil careers, if another man was to seize his military glory. Other talents could at a pinch be ignored, but that of a good general must belong to the emperor. Such were the worries that vexed him and over which he brooded in secret until he was tired – a sure sign in him of deadly purpose. Finally, he decided to store up his hatred for the present and wait for the first burst of acclaim and the enthusiasm of the army to die down. Agricola, you see, was still in possession of Britannia.

40. Domitian therefore gave orders that triumphal decorations, the honour of a splendid statue and all the other substitutes for a triumph should be voted to Agricola in the Senate, augmented by a most flattering address; further, the impression was to be conveyed that the province of Syria, then vacant through the death of the consular Atilius Rufus and reserved for men of senior rank, was intended for Agricola.[92] It was widely believed that a freedman in Domitian's closest confidence was sent with a letter offering Agricola Syria, but with instructions to deliver it only if he were still in Britannia. The freedman, it is said, met Agricola's ship in the very straits of the Ocean and without even hailing him returned to Domitian. The story may be true, or it may be a fiction, devised in keeping

with Domitian's character. Agricola, meanwhile, had handed over to his successor[93] a province peaceful and secure. In order not to publicize his arrival by the pomp of a crowded welcome, he avoided the attentions of his friends; by night he entered the city, and by night he went, as instructed, to the palace. He was welcomed with a perfunctory kiss and, without a word, dismissed to join the crowd of courtiers.

Anxious to tone down his military renown, irksome to civilians, by displaying other qualities he drank deep of peace and repose. He was modest in his dress, affable in conversation, never seen with more than one or two friends. As a result, the majority, who usually measure great men by their self-advertisement, after closely observing Agricola, were left asking why he was famous; few could read his secret aright.

41. Often during this period Agricola was denounced to Domitian behind his back, and as often behind his back acquitted. His danger did not arise from any charge against him or any complaint by an injured party, but from an emperor hostile to merit, his own renown and that deadliest type of enemy, the singers of his praises. And, indeed, the fortunes of the commonwealth in the years that followed were such as would not allow Agricola to be passed over in silence. One after another came the loss of all those armies in Moesia and Dacia, in Germania and Pannonia, through the rashness or cowardice of their generals; one after another came the defeats of all those experienced officers and the capture of all those cohorts.[94] No longer was it the frontier and the riverbank[95] that were in question, but the legionary headquarters and the maintenance of the empire. So, as loss was piled on loss, and year after year made notable by death and disaster, public opinion began to clamour for Agricola to take command. His energy, resolution and military experience were universally contrasted with the passivity and cowardice of the others. It is clear enough that Domitian's own ears were stung by the lash of such talk. The best of his freedmen spoke out of loyal affection, the worst out of malice and spleen, but all alike goaded on an emperor so ready to go wrong. And so Agricola, both by his own virtues and the vices of others, was driven headlong towards glory.

42. At last the year arrived in which Agricola was due to draw for the proconsulship of Africa or Asia,[96] and, with the execution of Civica still fresh in memory,[97] Agricola did not lack warning nor Domitian precedent. Some of the emperor's confidants approached Agricola in order to ask whether he really intended to take a province. They began somewhat slyly by praising the life of peaceful retirement, went on to promise their own assistance should Agricola care to decline, and at last with open threats and exhortations dragged him off to Domitian. The emperor, his hypocrite's part prepared, had assumed a majestic air; he listened to Agricola's request to be excused, and, after granting it, allowed himself to be thanked, with never a blush at so odious a favour. He did not, however, assign him the proconsular salary, usually offered in such cases and given by himself in some – perhaps from annoyance that Agricola had not asked for it, perhaps out of shame, lest he seem to have bought what he had forbidden. It is a distinctive feature of human nature to hate those whom you have harmed, and Domitian was especially prone to plunge into a fury that was all the more inexorable the more he kept it hidden. Yet even he was appeased by the restraint and good sense of Agricola, who declined to court, by a defiant and futile parade of freedom, the fame that must mean his fall. Let it be clear to those inclined to admire unlawful acts that even under bad emperors men can be great, and that a sense of duty and discretion, if backed by ability and energy, can reach that peak of honour that many have stormed by precipitous paths, winning fame, without serving country, through an ostentatious death.[98]

43. The end of his life was a bitter blow to us and a sorrow to his friends; to those outside his circle and even to complete strangers it was a matter of some concern. The general public as well, those mobs so busy with their own affairs, flocked to his house and discussed the news in the markets and clubs. When his death was announced no one exulted, no one forgot too readily. The sense of pity was increased by the persistent rumour that he had been poisoned.[99] We have no definite evidence – that is all I can say for certain. I would note, however, that throughout the whole of his illness there were more visits

from prominent freedmen and court physicians than is usual
with an emperor making calls by proxy; perhaps this was real
concern, perhaps mere prying. It was generally agreed that on
the day of his death the key stages in his decline were reported
by relays of runners, and no one could believe that tidings
brought so quickly would be unwelcome. However, Domitian
made a decent show of genuine sorrow; his hatred now was
satisfied, and he could always hide delight more readily than
fear. It is quite certain that at the reading of Agricola's will,
which made Domitian co-heir with his excellent wife and
devoted daughter, he was genuinely pleased and took it as a
well-judged compliment. So blinded and corrupted was his soul
with incessant flattery that he could not see that a good father
names as heir no emperor but a bad one.[100] *to prevent violence or jealousy*

44. Agricola was born on the Ides of June in the third consulship of Gaius Caesar; he died in his fifty-fourth year on the
tenth day before the Kalends of September in the consulship of
Collega and Priscinus.[101] Should posterity care to know what
he looked like, he was attractive rather than impressive. There
was no aggression in his features, but abundant charm of
expression. You could see at a glance that he was a good man,
you were tempted to believe him a great one. Cut off though he
was in the midst of his prime, measured by glory his life was
absolutely complete. He had wholly realized those true blessings that reside in a man's character, and having held the consulship and borne triumphal decorations what more could
fortune offer? He had no taste for bloated wealth, yet had a
handsome fortune. We may even count him blessed, who, leaving a wife and daughter to survive him, with his public position
unimpaired, his fame at its height and his kinsmen and friends
secure, avoided what was to come. Although he was not per-
mitted to see the dawn of this blessed age and the principate of
Trajan,[102] an event that he often foretold to us in prophecy and
prayer, he nevertheless had great compensation for his hastened
death. For he missed those last days, when Domitian no longer
left interval or breathing space, but, with a succession of blows
so continuous that they seemed a single one, exhausted the
strength of the commonwealth.

45. Agricola did not live to see the Senate House under siege, the senators hedged in by soldiers and that one fell stroke that sent so many consulars to death, so many noble ladies to exile and flight.[103] Only a single victory was yet credited to Carus Mettius, the screech of Messalinus was still confined to debate in the Alban fortress and Massa Baebius was at that very moment in the dock.[104] Soon, our hands led Helvidius off to prison, we were tortured by the looks of Mauricus and Rusticus, Senecio drenched us with his guiltless blood.[105] Nero at least averted his gaze; he did not inspect the crimes he ordered. It was distinctive to our torments under Domitian that we both watched and were watched: he noted down our every sigh and kept score as each of us turned pale, relying himself on that scowling ruddy visage with which he shielded himself from shame.

You were fortunate indeed, Agricola, in your glorious life, but no less so in your timely death. Those who were present at your final words attest that you met your death with a cheerful courage, as though doing your best to absolve the emperor of guilt. But your daughter and I have suffered more than the pang of a father's loss, for we grieve that we could not tend your illness, cheer your failing powers and take our fill of your look and embrace. We could not have failed to catch some last commands, some words to be engraved on our hearts for ever. This is our special sorrow, our peculiar hurt, that through the accident of our long absence from Rome we lost him four years before he died.[106] All, more than all, dear Father, was assuredly done to honour you by the devoted wife at your side; but there were tears due to you that were not shed and, as light failed, there was something for which your darkening eyes looked in vain.

46. If there is any mansion for the spirits of the just, if, as the wise aver, great souls do not perish with the body, quiet, O Father, be your rest! May you call us, your family, from feeble regrets and unmanly mourning to contemplate your virtues, which it would be a sin to mourn or lament. May we honour you in better ways – by our admiration and our praise, even, if our powers permit, by following your example. That is the true honour, the true devotion of souls knit close to yours. Your

daughter and wife I would urge to revere the memory of their
father and husband by pondering his words and deeds and by
cherishing the form and features of his mind above those of his
body. I would not ban completely likenesses in marble or
bronze. But the image of the human face, like that face itself, is
feeble and perishable, whereas the essence of the soul is eternal,
to be caught and expressed not through the substance and skill
of another, but only by individuals in their own lives. All that
we loved in Agricola, all that we esteemed, abides and shall abide
in the hearts of men, through endless ages, in the chronicles of
fame. For many men of old will be lost in oblivion, their name
and fame forgotten. Agricola's story has been told to posterity
and, so handed down, he will live.

GERMANIA

1. Germania is separated from the Gauls and from the Raeti and Pannonii by the Rhine and Danube rivers,[1] from the Sarmatians and Dacians[2] by the barrier of mutual fear or mountain ranges. The other parts, with their broad promontories and vast islands, are surrounded by the Ocean; in recent times war has revealed the existence there of nations and kings unknown before.[3] The Rhine rises in a remote and precipitous peak of the Raetian Alps and bends gently westward to lose itself in the northern Ocean. The Danube flows from a gentle and gradual slope of Mount Abnoba and passes more peoples than the Rhine in its course, before it discharges by six channels into the Pontic Sea. Its seventh mouth is swallowed up in marshes.

2. The Germani themselves, I am inclined to think, are natives of the land and very little affected by immigration or friendly interaction with other nations. For in ancient times those who wished to change their habitat travelled by sea and not by land, and the vast Ocean that lies beyond and, so to speak, defies intruders is seldom visited by ships from our world. Besides – to say nothing of the perils of a wild and unknown sea – who would leave Asia or Africa or Italy and seek out Germania, with its unlovely scenery and bitter climate, dreary to inhabit and even to behold, unless it were his home?

In their ancient songs, their only form of recorded history, the Germani celebrate the earth-born god Tuisto.[4] They assign to him a son, Mannus,[5] the author and founder of their race, and to Mannus three sons, after whom the people nearest the Ocean are named Ingvaeones, those of the centre Herminones, the remainder Istvaeones.[6] Some authorities, since the remote

"Mythical origins"
suggest he does not know
these *writers*
well

past invites guesswork, record more sons of the god and more national names, such as Marsi, Gambrivii, Suebi and Vandilii,[7] and those names are indeed genuine and ancient. As for the name 'Germania', it is modern and recently applied. The first people to cross the Rhine and oust the Gauls, those now called Tungri, were then called Germani.[8] It was the name of this nation, not that of a race, that gradually came into general use. And so, to begin with, they were all called Germani after the conquerors because of the terror these inspired, and then, once the name had been devised, they adopted it themselves.[9]

3. Hercules too is said to have visited them, and they sing his praises before those of other heroes on their way into battle.[10] They also have a different kind of song. By its delivery – *barritus*, they call it[11] – they kindle their courage and from the singing itself they forecast the result of the coming battle. They inspire or feel terror according to the sound of their battle-line, which they regard as a chorus of valour rather than voices. What they aim at most is a harsh tone and hoarse roar, and they put their shields before their mouths in order to make the voice swell fuller and deeper as it echoes back. Ulysses, too, in those long and fabled wanderings of his, is thought by some to have reached this Ocean and visited Germanic lands; they hold that he founded and named Asciburgium, a place on the banks of the Rhine still inhabited today.[12] They even add that an altar, consecrated by Ulysses and giving also the name of his father Laertes, was found long ago on that spot, and that certain monuments and barrows, inscribed with Greek letters, still exist on the borders of Germania and Raetia.[13] I am not disposed either to support such assertions by evidence or to refute them; my readers, as they are inclined, may either believe or disbelieve.

4. For myself, I accept the view of those who think that the peoples of Germania have never been tainted by intermarriage with other nations, and stand out as a race distinctive, pure and unique of its kind.[14] Hence the physical type, if one may generalize about so vast a population, is everywhere the same – wild blue eyes, reddish hair and huge frames that excel only in violent effort. They have no corresponding power to endure hard work and exertion, and little capacity to bear thirst and heat,

[handwritten: Racist theories of cultural differences. Cultural attributes attributed to race]

but their climate and soil have taught them to bear cold and *[crossed out]*
hunger.[15]

5. The country in general, while varying somewhat in character, either bristles with woods or festers with swamps. It is wetter where it faces Gaul, windier where it faces Noricum and Pannonia. Though fertile in grain crops, it is unfavourable to fruit trees.[16] It is rich in flocks, but they are mostly undersized. Even the cattle lack the natural honour and glory of their brows. It is numbers that please, numbers that constitute their only, their most dear form of wealth.[17] The gods have denied them gold and silver – in mercy or in wrath I cannot say. But I would not go so far as to assert that Germania has no lodes of silver and gold, for who has ever prospected? The Germani are unusually free of the desire to own and use these metals: one may see among them silver vessels, given as presents to their envoys and leading men, as lightly esteemed as earthenware.[18] *[handwritten: Not accurate]* The Germani nearest us, however, value gold and silver for their use in trade, and recognize and prefer certain types of our money; the peoples of the interior, truer to the plain old ways, employ barter. They like money that is old and familiar, denarii with the notched edge and the type of the two-horse chariot. They also seek out silver more than gold, not from any predilection, but because they find the larger number of silver coins more serviceable in buying cheap and common goods.[19]

6. There is not any abundance of iron, as may be inferred from the character of their weapons.[20] Only a few use swords or lances. The spears that they carry – *frameae* is the native word – have short and narrow heads, but are so sharp and easy to handle that the same weapon serves at need for close or distant fighting. The horseman asks for no more than his shield and spear, but the infantry also have javelins to shower, several per man, and hurl them to a great distance, either naked or lightly clad in cloaks. There is nothing ostentatious about their equipment; only the shields are picked out with carefully chosen colours. A few have breastplates, and just one or two helmets of metal or hide. Their horses are distinguished neither for beauty nor for speed, but also they are not trained in our fashion to execute various turns. They ride them

straight ahead or with a single swing to the right, keeping the
wheeling line so perfect that no one drops behind the rest. On
a general estimate, their strength lies more in infantry, and that
is why they fight in mixed groups.[21] Men who are fleet of foot
and admirably fit for cavalry combat are selected from all the
youth and stationed in the van. Their number is exactly fixed:
a hundred are drawn from each district, and 'the hundred' is
the name they bear at home. What began as a number becomes
a title of distinction. The battle-line is made up of wedge
formations. To retreat, provided that you return to the attack,
is considered crafty rather than cowardly. They bring in the
bodies of the fallen even when the battle hangs in the balance.
To throw away one's shield is the supreme disgrace; those so
disgraced are debarred from sacrifice or council, and many
who survive a battle have ended their shame with a noose.

7. They choose their kings for their noble birth, their leaders
for their valour. But even the power of the kings is not absolute
or arbitrary.[22] As for the leaders, it is their example rather than
their authority that wins them special admiration – their energy,
their distinction, or their presence in the front of the line. Moreover, no one is allowed to punish, to fetter or even to flog except
the priests, and not as punishment or on the leader's orders, but
as though in obedience to the god who they believe presides over
battle; they also carry into the fray figures and emblems taken
from their sacred groves.[23] A particularly powerful incitement to
valour is the fact that not chance nor the accident of mustering
makes the troop or wedge, but family and friendship. A man's
dearest possessions are close at hand; he can hear nearby the
laments of his women and the wails of his children. These are
the witnesses that a man reverences most, to them he looks for
his highest praise. The men take their wounds to their mothers
and wives, who are not afraid of counting and examining the
blows, and bring food and encouragement to those fighting.

8. Tradition has it that armies wavering and even on the
point of collapse have been restored by the steadfast pleas of
the women, who bared their breasts and described how close
they were to enslavement – a fate that the men fear more keenly
for their women than for themselves; it is even found that you

can secure a surer hold on a state if you demand among the
hostages girls of noble family. More than this, they believe that
there resides in women something holy and prophetic,[24] and so
do not scorn their advice or disregard their replies. In the reign
of Divus Vespasian we saw Veleda long honoured by many as a
divinity,[25] whilst even earlier they showed a similar reverence
for Aurinia[26] and others, a reverence untouched by flattery or
any pretence of turning women into goddesses.[27]

9. As for the gods, they worship Mercury above all, and consider it proper to win his favour on certain days even by human
sacrifices; Hercules and Mars they appease with the beasts
normally allowed.[28] Some of the Suebi sacrifice also to Isis.
I cannot determine the reason and origin of this foreign cult,
but her emblem, fashioned in the form of a Liburnian ship,
proves that her worship came in from abroad.[29] They do not,
however, deem it consistent with the divine majesty to imprison
their gods within walls or represent them with anything like
human features. They consecrate woods and groves, and they
call by the names of gods the hidden presence that they see only
by the eye of reverence.[30]

10. For divination and the casting of lots they have the highest possible regard. Their procedure in casting lots[31] is uniform.
They break off a branch of a fruit tree and slice it into strips;
they mark these by certain signs and throw them, as random
chance will have it, onto a white cloth. Then a state priest, if the
consultation is a public one, or the father of the family, if it is
private, prays to the gods and, gazing to the heavens, picks up
three separate strips and reads their meaning from the marks
scored on them. If the lots forbid an enterprise, there can be no
further consultation about it that day; if they allow it, further
confirmation by divination is required. The practice of consulting
the cries and flights of birds is of course known also to us;
peculiar to that people is the seeking of presentiments and
warnings from horses.[32] These horses are kept at public expense
in those sacred woods and groves; they are pure white and
undefiled by work for mortals. The priest and the king or leading man of the state yoke them to a sacred chariot and go along
with them, noting their neighs and snorts. No form of divination

inspires greater trust, not only among the commons, but also among the nobles and priests: they regard themselves as only the servants of the gods, but the horses as their confidants. There is yet another kind of divination used to forecast the issue of serious wars. They somehow secure a captive from the people with whom they are at war and match him against a champion of their own, each armed in native style. The victory of one or the other is taken as a precedent.

11. On matters of minor importance only the leading men debate, on major affairs the whole community; yet even where the commons have the decision, the matter is considered in advance by the leaders. Except in case of accident or emergency they assemble on fixed days, when the moon is either new or full; these, they hold, are the most auspicious times for embarking on new enterprises. They count not by days like us, but by nights;[33] it is by nights that they fix dates and make appointments. Night is thought to usher in the day. It is a defect of their freedom that they do not gather at once or in obedience to orders, but waste two or three days through their slowness to assemble. When the crowd so decides, they take their seats fully armed. Silence is then demanded by the priests, who on that occasion also have the right to enforce obedience. Then such hearing is given to the king or leading man as age, rank, military distinction or eloquence can secure; it is their prestige as councillors more than their power to command that counts. If a proposal displeases them, the people roar out their dissent; if they approve, they clash their spears.[34] No form of approval can carry more honour than praise expressed by arms.

12. One can launch an accusation before the council or bring a capital charge. The punishment varies to suit the crime. Traitors and deserters are hanged on trees; the cowardly, the unwarlike and those who disgrace their bodies are drowned in miry swamps under a cover of wicker.[35] The distinction in punishments implies that criminal deeds should be paid for publicly, but that shameful deeds should be hidden away. Even for lighter offences there are proportional penalties: those found guilty are fined a certain number of horses or cattle.[36] Part of the fine is paid to the king or state, part to the plaintiff or his

kin. In the same councils are elected the leaders who dispense justice through the country districts and villages. Each is attended by a hundred companions drawn from the commons, both to advise him and to add weight to his decisions.

13. No business, public or private, is transacted except under arms.[37] But it is the rule that no one shall take up arms until the state has attested that he will be worthy of them. Then in the public council one of the leading men or the father or a kinsman equips the young man with shield and spear. This, among the Germani, is the equivalent of our toga – the first public distinction of youth. They cease to rank merely as members of a household and are now members of the community. Conspicuous ancestry or great services rendered by their fathers can win the rank of leader even for mere lads. The others are attached to men who are more mature and approved, and no one blushes to be seen in the ranks of the companions.[38] This order of companions also has different grades, as determined by the leader, and there is intense rivalry among the companions to hold first place with the leader, among the leaders to have the most numerous and enthusiastic companions. Dignity and power alike consist in being always attended by a corps of chosen youths, a distinction in peace and protection in war. Nor is it only among a man's own people that he can win name and fame by the superior number and quality of his companions, but in neighbouring states as well; such men are courted by embassies and complimented by gifts, and often decide wars by their mere reputation.[39]

14. On the field of battle it is a disgrace to the leader to be surpassed in valour by his companions, to the companions not to equal the valour of their leader. To outlive one's leader by withdrawing from battle brings lifelong infamy and shame.[40] To defend and protect him, to attribute to his glory one's own brave deeds, that is the crux of their oath of allegiance: the leaders fight for victory, the companions fight for their leader. Many noble youths, if the land of their birth is stagnating from protracted peace and leisure, deliberately seek out other peoples that are then waging war. The Germani have no taste for peace; renown is more easily won among perils, and you

[handwritten margin note:] No distinction between "civil" & "military" sphere

cannot maintain a large body of companions except by violence and war. For the companions make demands on the generosity of their leaders, asking for 'that war horse' or 'that bloody and victorious spear'. As for the feasts, with their abundant if homely fare, these count simply as pay. Such open-handedness needs war and plunder to feed it. You would also find it harder to persuade them to plough the land and await its annual produce than to challenge a foe and earn the prize of wounds; indeed, they think it spiritless and slack to gain by sweat what they can buy with blood.[41]

15. When not engaged in warfare, they spend some little time in hunting, but more in idling, devoting themselves to sleep and gluttony. All the brave and fierce warriors do nothing at all; the care of house, hearth and fields is left to women, old men and the frailest of the family, while they themselves laze about. It is a remarkable inconsistency in their nature that they love indolence as much as they hate peace. It is customary for states to make voluntary and individual contributions of cattle or agricultural produce to the leaders. These are accepted as a token of honour, but also relieve their needs. The leaders take peculiar pleasure in gifts from neighbouring states, which are sent not only by individuals, but by the community as well: choice horses, splendid arms, metal discs and collars.[42] Now they have also learnt the practice of accepting money – from us.

16. It is well known that the peoples of Germania never live in cities, and cannot even bear houses set close together.[43] They live separately and apart, where spring, plain or grove has taken their fancy. Their villages are not laid out in our manner, with buildings adjacent or interlocked. Every man leaves an open space around his house, perhaps as a precaution against the risk of fire, perhaps because they are inexpert at building. They do not even use stone blocks or bricks; what serves their every purpose is unworked wood, both unimpressive and unattractive. Some parts of their houses they quite carefully smear with an earth so pure and brilliant that it looks like a painting or a coloured design. They also have the habit of hollowing out underground caves and heaping a great deal of dung on top; these serve as a refuge in the winter and as storage for their

crops. In such shelters they take the edge off the bitter frosts, and, should an invader come, he ravages the open country, but the secret and buried stores may pass altogether unnoticed or escape detection, simply because they have to be sought.

17. The universal dress is the short cloak,[44] fastened with a brooch or, failing that, a thorn; wearing no garment but this, they pass whole days by the hearth fire. The richest are distinguished by clothing that is not, as among Sarmatians and Parthians, loose and flowing, but tight and showing the shape of every limb.[45] They also wear the pelts of wild animals,[46] those near the Rhine without regard to appearance, those more distant with some refinement of taste, since they lack any finery that they can buy. The latter make careful choice of animal, then strip off the pelt and fleck it with patches from the skins of beasts that live in the outer Ocean and unknown seas. The dress of the women does not differ from that of the men, except that women often drape themselves with linen mantles that they adorn with purple and do not extend the upper part of their garment into sleeves, leaving the forearms and upper arms bare;[47] even the breast, where it comes nearest the shoulder, is also exposed. *Immodest by Roman standards*

18. For all that, marriage there is strict, and no feature of their culture deserves higher praise. They are almost unique among barbarians in being satisfied with one wife each; the very few exceptions involve men who, not because of sexual passion but because of high rank, receive offers of many wives. The dowry is brought not by wife to husband, but by husband to wife. Parents and kinsmen attend and approve the gifts, gifts not chosen to please a woman's whim or gaily deck a young bride, but oxen, a horse with reins, a shield with spear and sword.[48] For such gifts a man gets his wife, and she in her turn brings some present of arms to her husband: this they regard as the supreme bond, these the holy mysteries, these the deities of marriage. A woman must not imagine herself exempt from thoughts of manly virtues or immune from the hazards of war.[49] That is why she is reminded, in the very rites that bless her marriage at its outset, that she is coming to share a man's toils and dangers, that in peace and war alike she is to be his partner in all his sufferings and achievements. That is the meaning of the

team of oxen, of the horse equipped for a rider, of the gift of arms. It is on these terms that she must live her life and bear her children: that she is receiving something that she must hand over unspoilt and treasured to her children, for her son's wives to receive in their turn and pass on to her grandchildren.

19. Thus it is that they live lives of well-protected chastity, uncorrupted by the temptations of public shows or the excitements of banquets. Clandestine love-letters are unknown to men and women alike. For a nation so populous, adultery is rare in the extreme, and its punishment is summary and left to the husband. In the presence of kinsmen he shaves her hair and strips her, thrusts her from his house and flogs her throughout the village. There is no pardon for a woman who prostitutes her chastity; neither by beauty nor youth nor wealth can she find a husband. No one there finds vice amusing, or calls it 'up-to-date' to debauch and be debauched. Better still are those states in which only virgins marry, and the hopes and prayers of a wife are settled once and for all. They take one husband, just as they have one body or one life. No thought or desire must stray beyond him, so that they love not so much the husband as the married state. To restrict the number of children or to put to death any born after the first is considered criminal. Good morality is more effective there than good laws are elsewhere.[50]

20. In every home the children grow up, naked and dirty, to that strength of limb and size of body that excites our admiration. Every mother feeds her child at the breast and does not depute the task to maids and nurses.[51] The master is not distinguished from the slave by any pampering in his upbringing. They grow up together among the same flocks and on the same ground, until maturity sets apart the free and the spirit of valour claims them as her own. The young men are slow to mate, and their virility therefore is not exhausted. Nor are maidens rushed into marriage.[52] As old and full-grown as the men, they match their mates in age and strength, and the children reflect the might of their parents. The sons of sisters are as highly honoured by their uncles as by their own fathers. Some even regard this tie of blood as peculiarly close and sacred, and in taking hostages insist on it especially; they think that this gives them a firmer

grip on affections and a wider hold on the family. However, a
man's heirs and successors are his own children, and there is no
such thing as a will; where there are no children, the next to succeed are brothers and uncles, both paternal and maternal. The
larger a man's kin and the greater the number of his relations by
marriage, the stronger his influence when he is old; childlessness
has no reward.[53]

21. A man is bound to take up the feuds as well as the friend-
ships of father or kinsman. But feuds do not continue unrecon-
ciled. Even homicide can be atoned for by a fixed number of
cattle or sheep, and the whole family receives satisfaction.[54]
This is much to the advantage of the community, since private
feuds are particularly dangerous in conditions of freedom.

No other nation abandons itself more completely to banquet-
ing and entertainment. It is considered impious to turn any man
away from your door.[55] The host welcomes his guest with the
best meal that his means allow. When supplies run out, the man
who had been host becomes a comrade and a guide to hospitality: the two go uninvited to the nearest house. It makes no dif-
ference; they are welcomed just as warmly. No distinction is ever
made between acquaintance and stranger where the right to
hospitality is concerned. As the guest takes his leave, it is usual
to let him have anything he asks for; the host, as well, is no more
shy in asking. They take delight in presents, but ask no credit for
giving them and admit no obligation in receiving them. There is
a pleasant courtesy in the relations between host and guest.[56]

22. As soon as they rise from sleep, which they often pro-
tract well into the day, they wash in water that is usually warm;
can one wonder, where winter holds such sway? After washing,
they have a meal, with a separate place and a table for each.[57]
They then proceed to business or just as often banquets, always
armed. To drink away the day and night is not considered dis-
graceful. Brawls are common, as is normal among the intoxi-
cated, and are seldom settled by mere hard words, more often
by bloodshed and wounds. Nonetheless, they often at banquets
discuss such serious affairs as the reconciliation of enemies, the
forming of marriage alliances, the adoption of new leaders and
even the choice of peace or war. At no other time, they feel, is

Banquets are hot-beds of
political activities & canvassings

the heart so open to frank suggestions or so quick to warm to
a great appeal. A people neither canny nor cunning,[58] they take
advantage of the festivities to unburden themselves of their
most secret thoughts; every soul is uncovered and bare. The
next day brings reconsideration, and so due account is taken of
both occasions: they debate at a time that cuts out pretence,
they decide at a time that precludes mistake.[59]

23. For drink they extract a juice from barley or wheat,
which is fermented to make something like wine.[60] Those who
live nearest the Rhine can also get wine through trade. Their
food is plain – wild fruit, fresh game or curdled milk.[61] They
satisfy their hunger without any elaborate service or season-
ings. But they show no such self-control in drinking. You have
only to indulge their intemperance by supplying all that they
crave and you will gain as easy a victory through their vices as
through your own arms.

24. They have only one form of public show, which is the
same at every gathering. Naked youths, who do it for sport,
dance among swords and threatening spears. Practice produces
skill, and skill produces grace, but they do not perform for profit
or pay. However daring the play, their only reward is the pleasure they give the spectators. But dicing, if you can believe it, they
pursue in all seriousness and in their sober hours,[62] and are so
recklessly keen about winning or losing that, when everything
else is gone, they stake their personal liberty on the last decisive
throw. The loser goes into slavery without complaint; younger
or stronger he may be, but he suffers himself to be bound and
sold. Such is their perverse persistence, or 'honour', as they call
it. Slaves of this sort are sold and passed on, so that the winner
may be free of the shame that even he feels in his victory.

25. The ordinary slaves are not allotted, as is our custom, to
specific roles in the household; each has control of his own
house and home. The master imposes a fixed amount of grain,
cattle or clothing, as he would on a tenant, and up to this point
the slave obeys;[63] but domestic tasks as a whole are performed
by a man's wife and children. It is seldom that they flog a slave
or punish him with shackles or forced labour; they often kill
one, however, not in a spirit of stern discipline, but in a fit of

Similar to serfdom
not chattel

passion, as they might an enemy – except that the deed is unpunished. Freedmen rank little higher than slaves; they seldom have much influence in the household and never in the state, excepting only in nations that are ruled by kings: there they rise higher than free men and nobles.[64] With the rest, the inferiority of freedmen is the hallmark of liberty.

26. The practice of usury and compound interest is unknown; ignorance here is a surer defence than a ban. Lands in proportion to the number of cultivators are occupied by whole villages,[65] and then allotted in order of rank. The distribution is made easy by the vast extent of open land. They change their ploughlands yearly, and still there is ground to spare.[66] Their soil is fertile and plentiful, but they do not struggle to plant orchards, fence off meadows or water their gardens; the grain crop is their only levy on the earth. As a result, they divide the year into fewer seasons: winter, spring and summer are familiar to them as both ideas and words, but the name and gifts of autumn are alike unknown.[67] *no way*

27. There is no pomp about their funerals. The one rule observed is that the bodies of famous men are burned with special kinds of wood. When they have heaped up the pyre they do not throw robes or spices on top; only a man's arms, and sometimes his horse as well, are cast into the flames. The tomb is a raised mound of turf. They disdain to show honour by laboriously raising monuments of stone; these, they think, lie heavy on the dead. Weeping and wailing are soon over – sorrow and mourning linger. It is thought honourable for women to mourn, for men to remember.

Such is the general account that we have received of the origin and customs of the Germani as a whole. I must now set forth the institutions and practices of the individual nations, so far as they differ, and note the peoples that migrated out of Germania into Gaul.

28. That the Gauls were once more powerful is recorded by that greatest of authorities, Divus Julius;[68] and, in view of that, we may well believe that Gauls actually crossed into Germania.[69] For how paltry an obstacle was the river to prevent any nation that grew strong enough from seizing and continuing to seize

ever fresh lands, when these were still available to all and not yet partitioned between powerful kings! Thus, between the Hercynian Forest[70] and the rivers Rhine and Main, the Helvetii were settled,[71] and beyond them the Boii, both peoples of Gaul; the name Boihaemum still remains and indicates its ancient history, even after its change of inhabitants.[72] But whether the Aravisci came as immigrants to Pannonia from the Germanic nation of the Osi,[73] or the Osi from the Aravisci into Germania, cannot be determined; both speak the same language and have the same customs and character. Furthermore, of old, when both banks of the Rhine were equally poor and equally free, they offered identical advantages and disadvantages. The Treveri and Nervii[74] go out of their way to claim Germanic descent, as though so glorious an origin would clear them of any resemblance to the lacklustre Gauls. The actual bank of the Rhine is held by peoples of undoubted Germanic origin – the Vangiones, the Triboci and the Nemetes.[75] Even the Ubii, for all that they have earned the rank of Roman colony and prefer to be called Agrippinenses after the name of their founder, are not ashamed of their origin. They crossed the Rhine many years ago and, when their loyalty to us had been proved, were stationed right on the riverbank, not to be under surveillance, but to guard the gate against intruders.[76]

29. The most conspicuously courageous of all these peoples, the Batavi, do not hold much of the bank, but inhabit instead an island of the Rhine.[77] They were once a people of the Chatti, and as a result of civil war migrated to their present homes – destined there to become a part of the Roman empire. But the honour and distinction of their old alliance remain. They are not insulted by tribute or ground down by the tax-gatherer: free from taxes and special levies, and reserved for battle, they are like weapons and armour, 'only to be used in war'.[78] The same conditions apply to the nation of the Mattiaci;[79] for the greatness of Rome has spread the awe of its empire beyond the Rhine and the old frontiers. In geographical position they are on their own side, in heart and soul they are with us. For the rest, they are similar to the Batavi – except that their native soil and climate give their spirit a keener edge.

I am not inclined to reckon among the people of Germania those who cultivate the decumate lands,[80] settled though they may be beyond the Rhine and Danube. All the wastrels and penniless adventurers of Gaul seized on what was still no man's land. It was only later, when a frontier road was laid and garrisons brought forward, that they became a sort of projection of the empire and part of a province.

30. Beyond them dwell the Chatti,[81] from the Hercynian Forest onward, in a country less wide and marshy than the other states that Germania stretches out to form. For the hills run on and only gradually thin out, and the Hercynian Forest escorts the Chatti on their way and finally sets them down as it ends. This nation is distinguished by great physical hardiness, tautness of limb, savagery of expression and unusual mental vigour. They have, for Germani, plenty of judgement and acumen. They pick the men to lead them and obey the men they pick. They know how to keep their ranks, seize a chance or delay an attack. They map out the duties of the day and make sure the defences of the night. They regard fortune as uncertain, valour as certain. And something very uncommon and usually reserved for Roman discipline: they lay more stress on the general than on the army. Their strength lies entirely in their infantry, which, over and above its arms, has to bear the burden of tools and provisions. Other Germani may be seen going to battle, only the Chatti go to war. They seldom engage in sallies or chance engagements; such things really belong to cavalry, with its quick victories and its quick retreats. With infantry, speed comes close to cowardice, deliberate action tends towards endurance.

31. A custom that among other Germanic peoples is uncommon and depends on the enterprise of individuals has among the Chatti become a general rule: as soon as they come of age, they let their hair and beard grow long, and only clear their faces of this covering, which has been vowed and pledged to valour, when they have slain an enemy.[82] Over the bloodstained spoils they unbare their brows, for they say that only then have they paid the price of birth and shown themselves worthy of country and parents. The coward and the unwarlike remain unkempt. The bravest also wear an iron ring – which to the

Chatti implies disgrace – as a bond from which only the killing of an enemy can free them. Many of the Chatti like this fashion and even grow grey in this conspicuous state – marked out for friend and foe alike. With them it always rests to begin the battle; they are always in the front ranks, a startling sight. Not even in peace do they soften the savagery of their look. None of them has home or land or concerns of his own. To whatever host they choose to go, they get their keep from him, wasting the goods of others while despising their own, until old age drains their blood and makes them unequal to so harsh a form of heroism.

32. Next to the Chatti, along a Rhine that has now defined its channel and can serve as a boundary, live the Usipi and Tencteri.[83] The Tencteri, while sharing in the general military glory, excel in the art of skilful horsemanship. The infantry of the Chatti is not more renowned than the cavalry of the Tencteri. That is their inherited tradition, and that their descendants continue. The games of the children, the competitions of the young men, all take this same direction; even the old persist in it. Horses are handed down as part of the household, with its protecting gods and the rights of succession; the son who inherits them is not, as with the rest of the property, the eldest,[84] but the keenest and ablest soldier.

33. Next to the Tencteri once came the Bructeri,[85] but now the Chamavi and Angrivarii[86] are said to have taken their place. The Bructeri were ousted and almost annihilated by a league of neighbouring peoples. Perhaps they were hated for their arrogance, or it may have been the lure of booty, or else the gods were kind to Rome; indeed, they did not even begrudge us the spectacle of the battle.[87] Over 60,000 men fell, not by Roman swords and javelins, but, more splendid still, to gladden Roman eyes. Long, I pray, may foreign peoples persist, if not in loving us, at least in hating one another; for the imperial destiny drives hard, and fortune now has no better gift than the discord of our foes.[88]

34. The Angrivarii and Chamavi are shut in from behind by the Dulgubnii, Chasuarii and other peoples of no special note,[89] while in the front they are succeeded by the Frisii.[90] The Frisii are called the 'greater' and the 'lesser', in accordance with their

relative strength. Both nations have the Rhine as their border right down to the Ocean, and their settlements also extend around vast lakes, which have been sailed by Roman fleets. We have by that route even made assaults on the Ocean itself, and rumour has it that beyond there are pillars of Hercules still untried. Did Hercules really go there, or is it only our habit of assigning any outstanding achievement anywhere to that famous name? Drusus Germanicus was not deficient in daring, but the Ocean forbade further research into its own secrets or those of Hercules.[91] Since then no one has made the attempt, and it has been judged more pious and reverent to believe in what the gods have done than to investigate it.

35. This far towards the west we are familiar with Germania; to the north it recedes in a huge bend. The very first nation here is that of the Chauci.[92] They begin after the Frisii and hold a section of the coast, but they also lie along the flanks of all those nations that I have described, and finally curve back all the way to the Chatti.[93] This huge stretch of country is not merely occupied, but filled to overflowing by the Chauci. They are one of the noblest peoples of Germania, and one that actually prefers to maintain its greatness by acting justly. Free from greed and recklessness, they dwell in quiet seclusion, never provoking a war, never robbing or plundering their neighbours.[94] It is conspicuous proof of their valour and strength that their acknowledged superiority does not rest on aggression. Yet every man keeps his arms at hand, and, if occasion demands it, they have vast reserves of men and horses. So, even when they are at peace, their reputation remains the same.

36. On the flank of the Chauci and Chatti the Cherusci have been left free to enjoy an excessive and enervating peace – a pleasant but perilous indulgence amidst powerful aggressors, where there is no true peace. When the strong hand decides, restraint and integrity are words that belong to the victor. Thus the Cherusci, once the good and true, are now called slovenly and slack, while the luck of the victorious Chatti[95] has come to count as wisdom. In the fall of the Cherusci the neighbouring Fosi were also involved; they came second in prosperity, but got an equal share of adversity.

37. In the same peninsula of Germania, next to the Ocean, dwell the Cimbri,[96] a mighty name in history, though now just a tiny state. The traces of their ancient fame may still be seen far and wide in vast encampments on both sides of the Rhine, and by the size of these one still may gauge the mass and manpower of the nation and the historical truth of that great exodus. Rome was in its six hundred and fortieth year when the alarm of Cimbrian arms was first heard, in the consulship of Caecilius Metellus and Papirius Carbo. Reckoning from that year to the second consulship of the emperor Trajan, we get a total of just about two hundred and ten years:[97] so long is the conquest of Germania taking. In the course of that great span of time there have been many losses on each side. Neither the Samnites nor the Carthaginians, neither Hispania nor Gaul, not even the Parthians have taught us more painful lessons.[98] The freedom of Germania is a deadlier enemy than the despotism of Arsaces.[99] After all, with what has the East to taunt us except the slaughter of Crassus? And it soon lost Pacorus and was humbled at the feet of Ventidius.[100] But the Germani routed or captured Carbo, Cassius, Scaurus Aurelius, Servilius Caepio and Mallius Maximus, robbing the Roman people at almost a single stroke of five consular armies;[101] even from Caesar they stole Varus and his three legions.[102] Nor was it without painful loss that C. Marius smote the Germani in Italy, that Divus Julius smote them in Gaul, that Drusus, Nero and Germanicus smote them in their own lands.[103] But then the vast threats of Gaius Caesar ended in farce.[104] After that ensued a peace, until the Germani took advantage of our dissensions and civil wars to storm the headquarters of the legions and claim possession of Gaul.[105] Driven back once more, they have in recent times supplied us more with triumphs than with victories.[106]

38. We must now speak of the Suebi, who do not, like the Chatti or Tencteri, constitute a single nation. They occupy more than half Germania, and are divided into distinct peoples with distinct names, although all alike are called Suebi.[107] It is the special characteristic of this nation to comb the hair sideways and fasten it tight with a knot.[108] This distinguishes the Suebi from the other Germani; this, among the Suebi, distinguishes the free man from the slave. In other nations, either through some

kinship with the Suebi or, as often happens, through imitation, the practice exists, but is uncommon and confined to youth. But among the Suebi the bristling hair, even until it turns white, is twisted back[109] and often knotted on the very crown of the head. The leading men use an even more elaborate style. Such attention do they pay to their personal appearance – and yet in all innocence. It is not to seduce or attract seduction that they arrange their hair to such a height; they are adorned for the eyes of their enemies, to cause terror when they go into battle.

39. The Semnones[110] claim that they are the oldest and noblest of the Suebi, and confidence in their antiquity is bolstered by a religious rite. At a set time all the peoples who share that name and bloodline assemble through envoys in a wood hallowed by the auguries of their ancestors and the awe of ages. The public sacrifice of a human victim marks the grisly opening of their savage ritual. In another way, too, reverence is paid to the grove. No one may enter unless bound with a cord, as an inferior who acknowledges the might of the deity. Should he chance to fall, he must not get up on his feet again, but roll out over the ground. All this complex of superstition reflects the belief that in that grove the nation had its birth, and that there the god is ruler of all,[111] while everything else is subject to his sway. The prosperity of the Semnones has increased their authority: they inhabit a hundred country districts and, by virtue of their magnitude, count themselves chief of all the Suebi.

40. The Langobardi,[112] by contrast, are distinguished by the fewness of their numbers. Ringed round as they are by many mighty peoples, they find safety not in obsequiousness but in battle and its perils. After them come the Reudigni, Aviones, Anglii, Varini, Eudoses, Suarini and Nuitones,[113] behind their ramparts of rivers and woods. There is nothing noteworthy about these peoples individually, but they are distinguished by a common worship of Nerthus, or Mother Earth.[114] They believe that she interests herself in human affairs and rides among their peoples. In an island of the Ocean stands a sacred grove, and in the grove a consecrated cart, draped with a cloth, which none but the priest may touch. The priest perceives the presence of the goddess in this holy of holies and attends her, in deepest reverence, as her

cart is drawn by heifers. Then follow days of rejoicing and merry-making in every place that she deigns to visit and be entertained. No one goes to war, no one takes up arms; every object of iron is locked away; then, and only then, are peace and quiet known and loved, until the priest again restores the goddess to her temple, when she has had her fill of human company. After that, the cart, the cloth and, if you care to believe it, the goddess herself are washed clean in a secluded lake. This service is performed by slaves who are immediately afterwards drowned in the lake. Thus mystery begets terror and a pious reluctance to ask what that sight can be that only those doomed to die may see.

41. This section of Suebian territory extends into the more remote regions of Germania. Nearer to us, if we now follow the Danube as before we followed the Rhine, come the Hermunduri,[115] a state loyal to Rome. They are therefore the only Germani who trade with us not on the riverbank, but deep inside our borders, in the illustrious colony of the province of Raetia.[116] They come over where they will, and without a guard. To other nations we show only our arms and our camps; to them we open our homes and our villas – and they do not covet them. In the territory of the Hermunduri rises the river Elbe, a famous river once known in deed, but now by name alone.[117]

42. Next to the Hermunduri dwell the Naristi, followed by the Marcomani and Quadi.[118] The Marcomani are conspicuous in renown and power; they even won their land itself by their bravery, when they drove out the Boii.[119] Nor do the Naristi and Quadi fall below their high standard. These people form the front, so to speak, presented to us by Germania, where it is defined by the Danube. The Marcomani and Quadi down to our own times retained kings of their own race, the noble line of Maroboduus and Tudrus, but now they submit to foreigners too. The might and power of the kings depend upon the authority of Rome;[120] they sometimes receive the aid of our arms, more often of our wealth, but their strength is none the less.

43. The rear of the Marcomani and Quadi is enclosed by the Marsigni, Cotini, Osi and Buri.[121] Of these, the Marsigni and Buri recall the Suebi in language and mode of life. The Cotini and Osi are not Germani; that is proved by their languages, Gallic

in the one case, Pannonian in the other, and also by the fact that they submit to paying tribute. Part of the tribute is levied by the Sarmatians, part by the Quadi, who regard them as men of foreign blood; the Cotini, more to their shame, also mine iron.[122] All these peoples are settled in country with little plain, but plenty of uplands, mountain peaks and high ground. Suebia, in fact, is split down the middle by an unbroken range of mountains,[123] and beyond that live a great many peoples, among whom the name of the Lugii is the widest spread, covering as it does a number of states. I need only give the names of the most powerful – the Harii, Helvecones, Manimi, Helysii and Nahanarvali.[124] In the territory of the Nahanarvali there is shown a grove, hallowed from ancient times. The presiding priest dresses like a woman, but the gods, in Latin translation, are Castor and Pollux. That expresses the power of the divine presence; their actual name is Alci. There are no images, no trace of foreign superstition, but they are certainly worshipped as young men and brothers.[125] As for the Harii, they are superior in strength to the other peoples I have just mentioned; savage as they are, they enhance their innate ferocity by trickery and timing. They blacken their shields and stain their bodies and choose pitch-dark nights for their battles. The shadowy horror of this ghostly army inspires a mortal panic, for no enemy can stand so strange and devilish a sight. Defeat in battle always begins with the eyes.

44. Passing the Lugii, we find the Gotones[126] under the rule of kings: a rule slightly stricter than among the other Germanic peoples, but not yet beyond the bounds of freedom. Then, on the Ocean, are the Rugii and Lemovii.[127] All these peoples are distinguished by round shields, short swords and submission to regal authority.

Next are the states of the Suiones, amidst the Ocean itself,[128] which are strong not only in arms and men but also in fleets. The shape of their ships differs from the norm in having a prow at both ends, which is always ready to be put in to shore. They do not rig sails or fasten their oars in banks at the sides. Their oarage is loose, as on some rivers, and can be shifted, as need requires, from side to side.[129] Wealth, too, is held in high honour, and that is why they obey one ruler, with no restrictions and a claim to compliance that cannot be questioned. Arms are not, as among the other Germani, allowed to all and sundry, but are kept under custody, and the custodian is a slave. There are two reasons for this: the Ocean makes sudden invasions impossible, and armed men with nothing to do readily run riot. And of course it is not in the king's interest to assign control of arms to a noble or free man, or even a freedman.

45. Passing the Suiones, we find yet another sea that is sluggish and almost immobile.[130] This sea is believed to be the boundary that girds the earth, because the last radiance of the setting sun lingers here till dawn, with a brilliance that dims the stars. Rumour adds that you can hear the sound he makes as he leaves the waves and can see the shape of his horses and the rays on his head. Only so far – and the report seems true – does the world of nature extend.[131] Turning, then, to the right-hand shore of the Suebian Sea, we find it washing the territories of the Aestii,[132] whose rites and customs are those of the Suebi, but whose language is closer to Britannic. They worship the Mother of the Gods. As an emblem of the cult they wear images of boars, and this, instead of arms or human protection, ensures the safety of the worshipper even among his enemies. They seldom use iron weapons, but cudgels often. They cultivate grain and other crops with a patience unusual among the typically lazy Germani. Nor do they fail to ransack the sea; they are the only people to collect amber – *glesum* is their own word for it[133] – in the shallows or even on the beach. As you would expect of barbarians, they have never asked or discovered what it is or how it is produced. For a long time, indeed, it lay unheeded amidst the other jetsam, until our luxury made its reputation. They have no use for it themselves; they gather it crude, pass it on unworked and are astounded at the price they are paid. Amber, however, is certainly a gum of trees, as you may deduce from the fact that creeping and even winged creatures are often seen within it; these got caught in the sticky liquid, and were imprisoned as it hardened. Consequently, I suspect that in the islands and lands of the west, just as in the remote regions of the east where the trees sweat frankincense and balm, there must be woods and groves of unusual fertility. Their gums, drawn out by the rays of their near neighbour, the

sun, flow as a liquid into the adjacent sea and are washed by violent storms onto the opposite shores. If you care to test the properties of amber by applying fire to it, you will find that it lights like a torch and gives off a thick and fragrant flame; it then softens into something sticky, like pitch or resin.

Bordering on the Suiones are the nations of the Sitones.[134] They resemble them in all respects but one – they are ruled by a woman. Such is the extent of their decline, not merely below freedom, but even below decent slavery.

46. Here Suebia ends. I am uncertain whether to assign the nations of the Peucini, Veneti and Fenni to the Germani or the Sarmatians. The Peucini, however, who are sometimes called the Bastarnae,[135] in language, social habits, mode of settlement and dwelling are like Germani. All of them are squalid and their nobles slovenly; as a result of intermarriage they are taking on something of Sarmatian ugliness. The Veneti[136] have borrowed largely from Sarmatian ways; their plundering forays take them over all the wooded and mountainous country that rises between the Peucini and the Fenni. Nevertheless, they are to be classed as Germani, for they have settled houses, carry shields and are fond of travelling fast on foot; in all these respects they differ from the Sarmatians, who live in wagons or on horseback. The Fenni[137] are astonishingly wild and disgustingly poor. They have no arms, no horses, no homes. They eat wild plants, dress in skins and sleep on the ground. Their only hope is in their arrows, which, for lack of iron, they tip with bone. The same hunt provides food for men and women alike; for the women go everywhere with the men and claim a share in securing the prey. The only way they can protect their babies against wild beasts or rain is to hide them under a makeshift network of branches. To this the young men return, this is the haven for the old. Yet they count their lot happier than that of those who groan over field labour, sweat over house building and venture in hope and fear their own and other men's fortunes. They care for no one, man or god, and have gained the ultimate release: they have no needs, not even for prayer.

The rest is the stuff of fables – Hellusii and Oxiones[138] with the faces and features of men, but the bodies and limbs of animals. On such unverifiable stories I will express no opinion.

Glossary of Terms

auxiliaries Non-citizen troops, often from less developed parts of the empire, serving with the Roman army; from the reign of Augustus on they constituted a formal and permanent supplement to the citizen legions and were organized into formal units with fixed names.

centurion The chief professional officer in the Roman army, normally promoted from the ranks. There were normally six centurions in a cohort, each in command of a century of eighty men.

cognomen See 'names'.

cohort A Roman army unit; legions were divided into ten cohorts of 480 men each. Auxiliary infantry were also organized into cohorts of 500 men, under the command of a prefect.

colony A new foundation of Roman citizens established under the authority of officials in Rome; in the imperial period, it became increasingly common for indigenous towns to be given colonial status, sometimes with the addition of settlers from Italy, so that their inhabitants acquired Roman citizenship. In the late republican and early imperial periods, colonial foundations were often used to provide settlement for veterans.

commonwealth See 'Republic'.

consul The chief executive official in the Roman republican constitution; traditionally, two consuls were elected each year, so that the annual consulships could be used for dating purposes: 'in the consulship of so-and-so and so-and-so'. This practice continued in the imperial period, although the position of consul became largely honorary; it also became customary for the initial consuls of the year to resign before the end of their terms in favour of replacements (known as 'suffect consuls'). Men who had held the consulship were known as consulars; major provincial governorships were normally held by men of consular rank.

divus A Latin word meaning 'god', an alternative to the more common word *deus*; in the imperial period, it was used almost exclusively as a title for emperors who were officially deified after their deaths.

equestrian The equestrian order was the second tier of the Roman elite, ranking just below the senatorial order; men of equestrian rank had to possess property worth at least 400,000 sesterces. In the early imperial period equestrians began to fill an increasing number of administrative positions and military commands.

freedman In Roman tradition, a slave who had been freed by his owner became that person's freedman (or woman); freedmen were free Roman citizens, but had certain obligations to their former owners and often continued to work for them in some capacity.

legate A representative of a Roman official who exercised command under that official's authority. In the early empire, legates of praetorian rank often served as commanders of legions and as governors of lesser provinces under the direct authority of the emperor; more important provinces, such as Britannia, were governed by legates of consular rank.

legion Latin *legio*, the largest division of the Roman army. Only Roman citizens could serve in a legion; non-citizens served in the auxiliaries. By the late Republic, a legion nominally consisted of ten cohorts, each containing six centuries of eighty men, for a total strength of 4,800; the first cohort, however, seems normally to have been larger than the others. Under the emperors, each legion had its own commander and title, the latter normally consisting of a number and a name, e.g., Legio V Alauda.

names Traditional Roman names for men had three elements: first, the praenomen or personal name (e.g., Gnaeus); second, the nomen or family name (e.g., Julius); third, the cognomen, which usually distinguished a particular branch of the larger family (e.g., Agricola). The number of traditional praenomina was very small, and they were therefore normally abbreviated; the relevant ones are provided in the list of abbreviations. Tacitus sometimes follows contemporary fashion in inverting the order of the nomen and cognomen (e.g., 'Priscus Helvidius' at *Agr.* 2, 'Carus Mettius' and 'Massa Baebius' at *Agr.* 45). Women traditionally had only one name, the nomen with the feminine ending, although in the imperial period they began to have two names, the second derived from a cognomen or some other family name (e.g., Domitia Decidiana).

patrician An elite hereditary status in Rome. In archaic Rome patricians monopolized the most powerful public offices, but by the late Republic only a few largely ceremonial positions were reserved for them. Emperors had the right to confer patrician status on people as a mark of honour.

pontifex   A member of one of the main colleges of public priests in Rome; the pontifices had general oversight of public cults, the calendar and burial law. The president of the college was the pontifex maximus, a position always held by the emperor from Augustus on.

praenomen   See 'names'.

praetor   The second highest of the civic officials in the Roman republican constitution; praetors traditionally had particular oversight over judicial matters. Augustus set the number of praetors at twelve a year, only some of whom were allotted judicial roles. Their other duties included financing some of the games that took place during the major religious festivals at Rome. Men of praetorian rank, those who had held the praetorship, often went on to command a legion or govern one of the less important provinces.

prefect   A title (Latin *praefectus*) applied to a number of different civic officials and military officers, including the commanders of cohorts and of fleets.

proconsul   A title given in the imperial period to anyone who exercised consular power without holding the actual office of consul at that time; it was particularly used of men who governed provinces under the control of the Senate, as opposed to legates, who were representatives of the emperor.

procurator   A Latin word simply meaning 'supervisor', used for a variety of officials, mostly of equestrian status; the most important were the non-senatorial governors of certain provinces (such as Egypt) and the emperor's financial agents in provinces like Britannia that had governors of senatorial status.

province   One of the various subdivisions of the empire, governed by Roman officials.

quaestor   The lowest ranked of the major civic officials in the Roman republican constitution; from 81 BC on there were normally twenty quaestors elected each year. Quaestors generally served as assistants to senior magistrates, either in Rome or in a province.

Republic   From Latin *res publica*, 'commonwealth', the phrase most frequently used by Roman writers to refer to the Roman state. In modern scholarship, the term 'Republic' is used in particular of the period prior to Augustus and the establishment of one-man rule, when executive power lay in the hands of annually elected magistrates.

Senate   A deliberative body in Rome consisting in practice of all current and former civic officials. Under the Republic, although the Senate's role was in theory merely advisory, it acted in effect as the chief policy-making body; under the emperors its effective power was considerably reduced, although senators continued individually and collectively to play a major role in administration and to constitute the social elite of the empire.

suffect consul See 'consul'.

tribune This title was used of two different positions. A tribune of the people was a civic official in the Roman republican constitution, charged especially with upholding the rights of the people; ten tribunes were elected each year. A tribune of the soldiers, or military tribune, was an officer of the Roman army, serving just below the legionary commander; there were normally six to a legion. The position of military tribune was normally held by young men at the start of their careers; the senior tribune in a legion was marked for a senatorial career (*tribunus laticlavius*), the others for equestrian careers.

triumph A major Roman ceremony in which a general who had won an important victory processed with his troops through the city to the temple of Jupiter on the Capitol. In the imperial period, when the right to celebrate a triumph was limited to emperors and members of their immediate families, it became customary to award other victorious commanders the decorations worn by a triumphing general, in lieu of an actual triumph.

MAPS

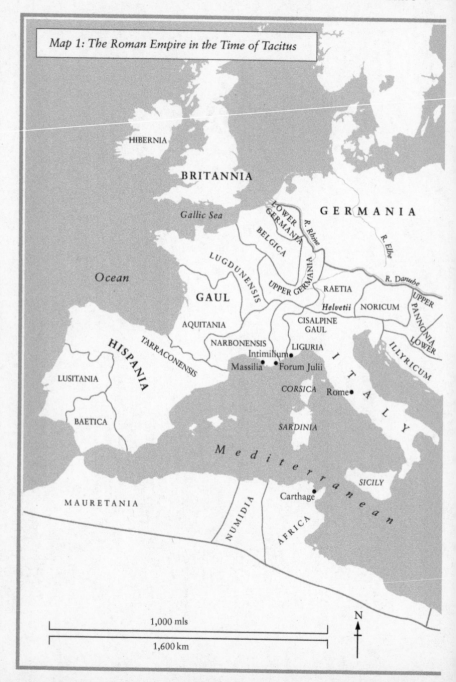

Map 1: The Roman Empire in the Time of Tacitus

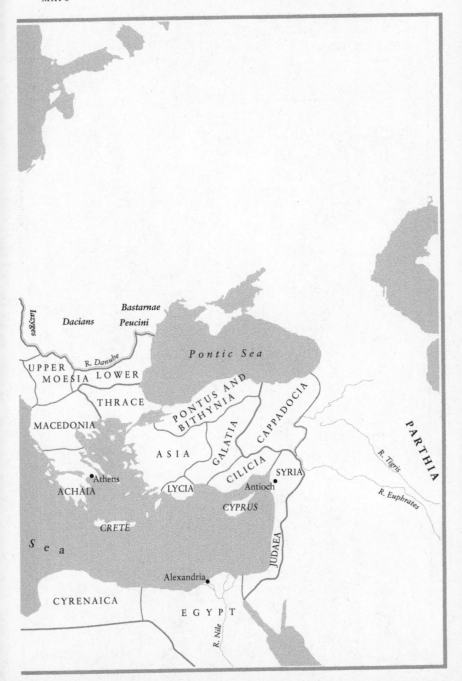

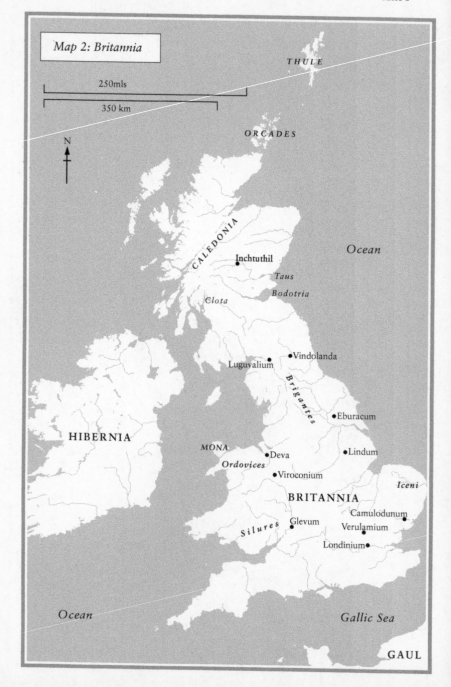

Map 2: Britannia

250mls

350 km

N

THULE

ORCADES

CALEDONIA

Inchtuthil

Taus

Bodotria

Clota

Ocean

Vindolanda

Luguvalium

Brigantes

Eburacum

HIBERNIA

MONA

Deva

Ordovices

Viroconium

Lindum

BRITANNIA

Iceni

Silures

Glevum

Camulodunum

Verulamium

Londinium

Ocean

Gallic Sea

GAUL

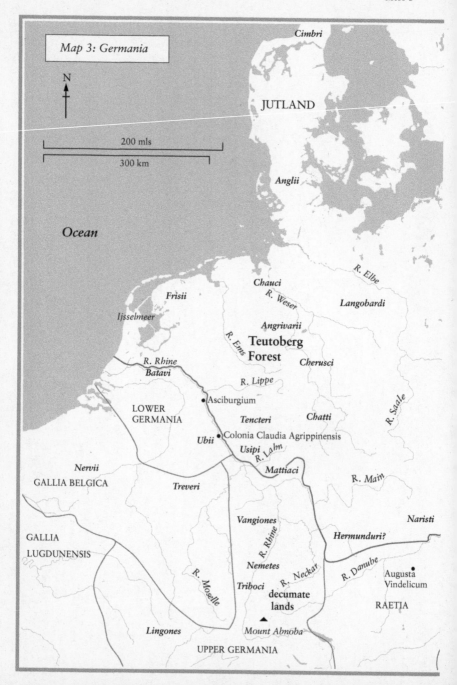

Map 3: Germania

N

200 mls

300 km

Ocean

Cimbri

JUTLAND

Anglii

Chauci

R. Elbe

Frisii

R. Weser

Langobardi

Ijsselmeer

Angrivarii

R. Ems

Teutoberg
Forest

Cherusci

R. Rhine

Batavi

R. Lippe

R. Saale

•Asciburgium

LOWER
GERMANIA

Tencteri

Chatti

Ubii

•Colonia Claudia Agrippinensis

Usipi

R. Lahn

Nervii

Mattiaci

R. Main

GALLIA BELGICA

Treveri

Vangiones

Naristi

GALLIA
LUGDUNENSIS

R. Rhine

Hermunduri?

Nemetes

R. Neckar

R. Danube

Augusta
Vindelicum

R. Moselle

Triboci

decumate
lands

RAETIA

Lingones

Mount Abnoba

UPPER GERMANIA

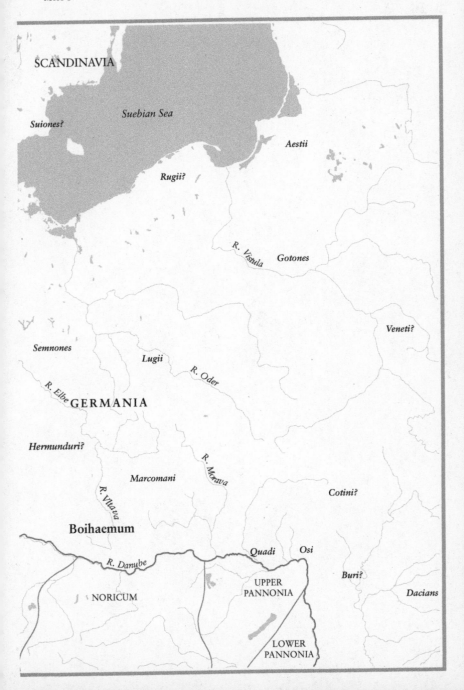

NOTES

All dates are AD unless specified otherwise.

Notes to *Agricola*

1. *Rutilius and Scaurus told theirs*: Important political figures in Rome during the late second and early first centuries BC. P. Rutilius Rufus, as proconsul of Asia, attempted to control the activities of the tax collectors, who took their revenge in 92 BC by accusing him of extortion; he was convicted and went into exile in the very province that he had been accused of plundering, where he wrote an autobiographical account of his times. M. Aemilius Scaurus became consul and leader of the Senate in 115 BC, and was a dominant figure for the next twenty years; he published three volumes of memoirs that were admired by Cicero (*Brutus* 112).

2. *beg an indulgence*: Some scholars think that this refers to an unsuccessful attempt to obtain approval for his project from Domitian.

3. *of Paetus Thrasea ... by Herennius Senecio*: P. Clodius Thrasea Paetus was a distinguished senator in the reigns of Claudius and Nero; opposed to the Senate's increasingly servile behaviour under Nero, he withdrew completely from public life and after being charged with treason committed suicide in 66 (Tac. *Ann.* 16.21–35). C. Helvidius Priscus, Thrasea Paetus' son-in-law, violently criticized the emperor Vespasian and was put to death in 75 (Suet. *Vesp.* 15). Q. Junius Arulenus Rusticus, who as a young man had tried to prevent Thrasea's execution (Tac. *Ann.* 16.26.4–5), and Herennius Senecio wrote laudatory accounts of their respective deaths, for which in 93, under Domitian, they were prosecuted for treason and put to death (Suet. *Dom.* 10.3, Dio 67.13.2). See Introduction C2, and *Agr.* 45 with nn. 103–5.

4. *triumviri*: The *triumviri capitales*, a board of three minor magistrates with responsibility for executing the sentences in cases involving capital charges.

5. *the Comitium and the Forum*: The Forum was the main space for public business in Rome, located in the heart of the city; the Comitium was traditionally the chief place for political assemblies, off the western end of the Forum in front of the Senate House.

6. *were banished*: That Domitian expelled philosophers from Rome is well attested (Plin. *Ep.* 3.11.2, *Pan.* 47.1; Suet. *Dom.* 10.3; Dio 67.13.3); both Suetonius and Dio imply that the order was connected with the prosecutions of Arulenus Rusticus and Herennius Senecio in 93.

7. *Nerva Caesar ... Nerva Trajan*: The emperor Nerva and his adopted son, Trajan. The forms of the names suggest that Tacitus was writing this passage after late October 97, when M. Ulpius Traianus was adopted by Nerva and took the name Imperator Caesar Nerva Traianus, but before 27 January 98, when Nerva died and was officially deified as Divus Nerva.

8. *fifteen years ... cruelty of the emperor*: Tacitus is referring to the reign of Domitian (81–96), who in his later years put many leading men to death; see further *Agr.* 45 with nn. 103–5.

9. *Forum Julii*: Modern Fréjus, on the southeast coast of France. It is first mentioned in a letter of May 43 BC (Cicero, *Letters to his Friends* 10.15.3), and so must originally have been founded by Julius Caesar; Augustus later refounded it as a colony of Roman veterans and a naval base (Plin. *NH* 3.35, Tac. *Ann.* 4.5.1). Agricola's family name Julius suggests that his paternal ancestor had been granted Roman citizenship by either Caesar or Augustus, and was thus possibly a native of the region rather than a settler from Italy. For the date of his birth, 13 June 40, see *Agr.* 44 with n. 101. It is likely that he was actually born at Rome, where his father was buried (see n. 11 below).

10. *equivalent of nobility in the equestrian order*: The Latin word *nobilis*, literally 'well-known', was used to designate someone of senatorial status whose ancestors had held high public office; Tacitus means that in the equestrian order the holding of important procuratorships conferred the same sort of distinction. Nothing else is known of Agricola's grandfathers.

11. *eloquence and philosophy*: L. Julius Graecinus is known from references in several early imperial writers as well as an epitaph erected by his brother (*AE* 1946, no. 94 = *CIL* VI.41069), which indicates that he reached the office of praetor. Seneca records

a clever comment of his about a contemporary philosopher (*Epistles* 29.6), and the agricultural writer Columella praises his two-volume study of viticulture as 'witty and learned' (*On Agriculture* 1.1.14).

12. *Marcus Silanus ... lost his life for refusing*: Two men named M. Junius Silanus are known from the reign of Gaius (Caligula). One, the father of Gaius' first wife (suffect consul in 15), was forced to commit suicide in 37 (Dio 59.8.4); the other (consul in 19) is known to have been regarded by Gaius with fear and suspicion when he was serving as proconsul of Africa, probably in the period 29–35 (Tac. *Hist.* 4.48.1); it is not clear which man is meant. Seneca (*On Benefits* 2.21.5) says that Graecinus was killed 'for this reason alone, that he was a better man than is expedient for a tyrant that anyone be'; his death must have been within months of Agricola's birth in June 40, since Gaius was assassinated on 24 January 41.

13. *Massilia ... happy blend*: Modern Marseilles, on the southeast coast of France. It was settled *c.* 600 BC by Greek colonists and maintained its Greek character well into the imperial period. Romans from the provinces were generally regarded as more strict and frugal than those from Rome itself.

14. *Suetonius Paulinus*: C. Suetonius Paulinus was governor of Britannia in 58–61 (see further *Agr.* 14–16); Agricola served under him as *tribunus laticlavius*.

15. *veterans butchered ... armies isolated*: A reference to the revolt of Boudicca in 60–61; see Introduction A5, and *Agr.* 16 with n. 54.

16. *an illustrious house*: An inscription (*ILS* 966) reveals that a Domitius Decidius, probably her father, was chosen by the emperor Claudius to be one of the quaestors in the charge of the treasury, and later held the praetorship.

17. *his proconsul*: L. Salvius Otho Titianus, the brother of the future emperor Otho, was proconsul of Asia in 63–4; Tacitus elsewhere (*Hist.* 2.60.2) says that when Otho's enemy Vitellius came to power he regarded Titianus as so worthless that he did not even bother to have him killed.

18. *no sacrilege but Nero's*: After the great fire in Rome in 64, Nero had raised funds by plundering the treasure from temples in both Rome and the provinces (Tac. *Ann.* 15.45). Since Tacitus here makes it clear that this treasure was not restored, other people must have taken advantage of the circumstances to steal treasures for themselves.

19. *Otho's fleet ... the Intimilians*: An episode from the civil wars of 69. The town of Intimilium (mod. Ventimiglia, on the northwest coast of Italy) was some 55 miles east of Forum Julii. Probably in March, the emperor Otho sent a fleet-based expedition into this region to prevent troops loyal to his rival Vitellius from crossing the Alps into Italy, but his soldiers instead engaged in indiscriminate plunder and destruction; see further Tac. *Hist.* 2.12–13 (where he calls Intimilium by the alternative name Albintimilium).

20. *Mucianus*: C. Licinius Mucianus, while governor of Syria (67–9), had urged Vespasian to undertake his attempt to become emperor and served as his de facto representative in Rome until Vespasian's own arrival there in the late summer of 70.

21. *Twentieth Legion*: In Britannia, one of the legions that took part in the original invasion of Britannia; it had been stationed at Glevum (mod. Gloucester), although it was at this time apparently moved to Viroconium (mod. Wroxeter). Its 'disloyal' commander was M. Roscius Coelius; see further *Agr.* 16 with n. 58.

22. *Vettius Bolanus*: Governor 69–71; see further *Agr.* 16 with n. 59.

23. *Petilius Cerialis*: Governor 71–3; see further *Agr.* 17 with n. 60.

24. *province of Aquitania*: A province in southwestern Gaul. This appointment, and even more the promotion to patrician rank, are clear signs of imperial favour; it is uncertain whether this was due solely to Agricola's loyalty and talents or also to some personal connection with the imperial house that Tacitus chose not to mention.

25. *position and peoples of Britannia*: Chapters 10–12 constitute a miniature ethnography of Britannia; such ethnographic digressions were a standard feature of ancient historical works. See Introduction D1.

26. *Hispania on the west*: This erroneous notion was widespread (Caes. *Gall.* 5.13.2, Plin. *NH* 4.102).

27. *Livy and Fabius Rusticus*: The Roman historian Livy, who wrote under Augustus, is known to have described Britannia in the now-lost Book 105 of his history, in connection with Julius Caesar's invasions of Britannia in 55 and 54 BC. Fabius Rusticus was a historian of the first century AD whose work, also now lost, was later used by Tacitus in his account of the reign of Nero (*Ann.* 13.20.2, 15.61.3); the context in which he discussed Britannia is not known.

28. *elongated diamond ... double-bladed axe*: The precise meaning of these terms is uncertain. R. M. Ogilvie and I. Richmond (*Cornelii*

Taciti De Vita Agricolae (Oxford: Clarendon Press, 1967), pp. 168–70) argued that the Latin word *scutula*, translated here as 'diamond', should be emended to *scapula*, 'shoulder-blade', and that *bipennis*, literally a double-headed axe, is here simply a poetic word for an ordinary axe; if so, both words would indicate a rough triangle with two long sides.

29. *proving that Britannia was an island*: The voyage to which Tacitus refers took place in 83, near the end of Agricola's final year as governor (*Agr.* 38). This accomplishment of Agricola's was still emphasized by Dio (39.50.4 and 66.20.1), writing well over a century later.

30. *hitherto unknown islands called the Orcades*: The Orkneys, which were in fact known at least by the 40s, when they are mentioned by Mela (3.54; cf. Plin. *NH* 4.103). Nevertheless, Agricola's subjugation of them made enough of an impression to be noted some thirty years later by Juvenal (2.160–61).

31. *Thule*: This island was first mentioned by the Greek navigator Pytheas, who in the late fourth century BC voyaged in the seas north of Europe; he described it as lying six days' sail north of Britannia near the 'congealed sea' (Strabo 1.4.2, Plin. *NH* 2.187). Pytheas' Thule was perhaps Iceland, but most scholars agree that Tacitus is here applying the name to Shetland.

32. *sluggish ... as other seas do*: Stories about a 'congealed sea' in the far north went back to Pytheas (see previous note; cf. Plin. *NH* 4.104), but Tacitus is here more likely describing the experience of ships attempting to sail into the North Atlantic Current, which passes close to the western shores of Shetland. See also his reference to a 'sluggish and almost immobile' sea north of Germania (*Germ.* 45).

33. *Germanic origin*: On the physical characteristics of the Germani, see *Germ.* 4 with n. 14.

34. *situation under the heavens*: Tacitus could have in mind either the notion that climatic conditions determine physical types (Vitruvius, *On Architecture* 6.1.3–11) or the astrological theory that different stars and planets are powerful in different regions and determine the characters of those who live in them (Manilius, *Astronomica* 4.696–743; Ptolemy, *Tetrabiblos* 2.3); for many people in antiquity the two ideas were probably interconnected. See Introduction D1.

35. *boldness in courting danger ... cowardice in avoiding it*: A commonplace in the Roman characterization of the Gauls; see, for example, Caes. *Gall.* 3.19.6.

36. *as the Gauls once were*: The notion that exposure to civilization made barbarians less warlike and more docile was widespread in ancient thought; see, for example, Caes. *Gall.* 1.1.3 and especially 6.24 (a passage to which Tacitus refers at *Germ.* 28). According to Tacitus, Agricola deliberately exploited this principle in order to pacify Britannia (*Agr.* 21).

37. *fight with chariots*: Described in detail by Caesar (*Gall.* 4.33).

38. *inability to cooperate*: Caesar describes the Gauls on the mainland in very similar terms (*Gall.* 6.11); Tacitus elsewhere expresses his appreciation for the benefits that the Romans derive from the divisions among their enemies (*Germ.* 33).

39. *fails to reach the sky and its stars*: Tacitus' meaning here is not very clear, but he seems to have thought that night is a shadow cast by the earth; around its edges, where there is nothing but Ocean, the earth is too flat to cast much of a shadow, and hence the darkness of night does not extend as high into the sky. His observation about the short nights of course applies only to the summer.

40. *Red Sea*: The Romans used this term not only for what is now known as the Red Sea, but also for the Persian Gulf and the Indian Ocean more generally; it is not clear what in particular Tacitus had in mind here.

41. *Divus Julius ... to posterity*: Caesar invaded Britannia in 55 BC and again in 54 BC (Caes. *Gall.* 4.20–36 and 5.8–23); although on both occasions he won victories and took hostages from local leaders, for many years thereafter the only follow-up was diplomatic rather than military. See Introduction A2.

42. *'precedent'*: Tacitus is here probably alluding to Augustus' posthumous advice not to extend the borders of the empire any further (Tac. *Ann.* 1.11.4), a policy that Tiberius carefully maintained. In fact, Britannia was apparently not entirely out of Augustus' thoughts: Dio claims that in the early part of his reign Augustus several times contemplated an invasion of Britannia (49.38.2, 53.22.5 and 25.2; cf. Horace, *Odes* 1.35.29–30 and 3.5.2–4), and he certainly maintained Rome's diplomatic involvement in Britannic affairs (Strabo 4.5.3; Augustus, *Achievements* 32.1); see Introduction A3.

43. *came to naught*: Gaius was involved in military activity in northern Europe for some nine months in 39–40; whatever his plans may have been, later writers present the whole episode as a farce (Suet. *Calig.* 43–8, Dio 59.21.1–3), and Tacitus makes similarly dismissive comments elsewhere (*Germ.* 37, *Hist.* 4.15.2); see

Introduction A4. A planned invasion of Britannia is sometimes thought to lie behind the bizarre story that Gaius drew up his army on the shore of the North Sea and then ordered them to collect seashells as 'plunder from the sea' (Suet. *Calig.* 46, Dio 59.25.1–3).

44. *Divus Claudius ... Vespasian as his colleague*: In the summer of 43; the overall commander was A. Plautius, although Claudius briefly joined the force in person (Suet. *Claud.* 17, Dio 60.19–21); see Introduction A4. Vespasian was the commander of Legio II Augusta and had enough success to earn triumphal decorations (Suet. *Vesp.* 4).

45. *Aulus Plautius*: He continued on as first governor after leading the invasion in 43. When he returned to Rome in 47, Claudius awarded him an ovation, a lesser version of the triumph; Plautius was the only general from outside the imperial family to be granted this honour after the reign of Augustus (Suet. *Claud.* 24.3, Tac. *Ann.* 13.32.2).

46. *Ostorius Scapula*: He succeeded Plautius as governor in 47; over the course of the next six years he put down an uprising by the Iceni in Norfolk, dealt with a disturbance among the Brigantes in Yorkshire and initiated the Roman advance into Wales. It was to him that Cartimandua, the queen of the Brigantes, turned over Caratacus, a major leader of the resistance against Roman conquest; he was fighting against the Silures in southern Wales when he died in 52 (Tac. *Ann.* 12.31–9).

47. *colony of veterans was founded*: Camulodunum, mod. Colchester, founded probably in 49.

48. *King Togidumnus*: Also known from a fragmentary inscription from Chichester (*RIB* 1.91, as emended in *AE* 1979, no. 382), which describes him as 'Ti. Claudius [To]gidubnus, Great King in Britannia'; it is apparent from this that he had received Roman citizenship, probably from the emperor Claudius. The exact form of his name is uncertain. The variation between '-dumnus' and '-dubnus' is common in Latin transliterations of Celtic names; more problematic is the fact that the chief manuscript of *Agricola* gives the name as 'Cogidumnus', although the variant 'Togidumnus' is noted in the margin. The latter is more likely to be correct, since Celtic names beginning with 'Togi-' are much better attested than those beginning with 'Cogi-'.

49. *Didius Gallus*: Governor 52–7. Shortly before his arrival the Silures had defeated a Roman legion under C. Manlius Valens, who had apparently carried on with the war against them when

Ostorius Scapula died (see n. 46 above). Gallus began by continuing actions against the Silures, but was soon called away to deal with problems among the Brigantes, where Venutius, the former husband of queen Cartimandua, was trying to stir up a rebellion against her (Tac. *Ann.* 12.40; cf. 14.29.1); his accomplishments were perhaps more significant than Tacitus suggests.

50. *Veranius*: Governor in 57–8; Tacitus elsewhere (*Ann.* 14.29.1) says that he too campaigned against the Silures. His earlier career is known from an inscription (*AE* 1953, no. 251 = *CIL* VI.41075), which records that he had served as the first governor of Lycia in what is now southern Turkey after its annexation in 43 and went on to be consul in 49; it was presumably his experience with pacifying native peoples in newly acquired mountainous regions that led Nero to appoint him governor of Britannia.

51. *Suetonius Paulinus*: Governor 58–61 (the name is spelt Paullinus in inscriptions); we have no details about his 'two years of success', but they probably involved the expansion of Roman control in Wales, culminating in his attack on Mona (mod. Anglesey) in 60. Tacitus elsewhere (*Ann.* 14.29–30) reports on that campaign in more detail, describing Mona as 'a sanctuary for refugees', presumably from Suetonius' actions elsewhere in Wales.

52. *in the telling*: The speech that follows, which in the original Latin is in reported rather than direct speech, is simply a composition of Tacitus enumerating the sorts of grievances that newly subjugated peoples might be thought to have. Elsewhere he indicates that the specific cause of the revolt was the greed and brutality of the Roman officials and soldiers who were bringing the territory of the Iceni under direct Roman rule after the death of their king Prasutagus (*Ann.* 14.31).

53. *threw off the yoke*: The reference is to Arminius' massacre of three legions under P. Quinctilius Varus in 9, which effectively ended Roman attempts to extend the empire beyond the Rhine. See Introduction A3, and *Germ.* 37 with n. 102.

54. *Boudicca*: The widow of Prasutagus (see n. 52 above); for more detailed accounts of her revolt, see Tac. *Ann.* 14.32–7 and Dio 62.1–12. The original form of her name was probably 'Boudica', related to a Celtic word meaning 'victory', although in modern times it became familiar as 'Boadicea'. To say that 'the whole island' revolted is probably an exaggeration: it centred on the Iceni, although others may have joined in.

55. *no distinction of sex in the appointment of leaders*: In fact, the only other female ruler among the Britanni known to us is

Cartimandua of the Brigantes, and according to Tacitus (*Ann.* 12.40.3) her people finally rebelled against her because they were unwilling to be 'subjected to the rule of a woman'; see further n. 59 below.

56. *the colony itself*: That is, Camulodunum; see the detailed account in Tac. *Ann.* 14.31–2, in which the temple of Divus Claudius is noted as a particular object of resentment; archaeological remains of burnt and melted glassware, pottery and coins attest to the destruction of the town. Tacitus does not mention here the attacks on Londinium (mod. London) and Verulamium (mod. St Albans).

57. *Petronius Turpilianus*: Governor 61–3. Tacitus refers elsewhere to his governorship in equally curt and dismissive terms (*Ann.* 14.39.3), and there is no further evidence. Turpilianus' chief goal, however, must have been to restore order and security, not to extend Roman rule; see Introduction A5.

58. *Trebellius Maximus*: Governor 63–9. The civil wars to which Tacitus refers began in March 68; see Introduction A5. It was shortly thereafter, it seems, that the mutiny against Trebellius broke out, fanned, as Tacitus informs us elsewhere (*Hist.* 1.60), by M. Roscius Coelius, the legate of Legio XX Valeria; cf. *Agr.* 7 with n. 21. Trebellius ended by fleeing to Vitellius about the time the latter became emperor in April 69.

59. *Vettius Bolanus*: Governor 69–71; initially appointed by Vitellius, he was kept in his post until Vespasian had consolidated his rule. Since Bolanus had to contend with the aftermath of the mutiny against Trebellius Maximus as well as the loss of 8,000 men sent to support Vitellius (Tac. *Hist.* 2.57.1), any 'lack of action in face of the foe' would have been understandable. But Tacitus' complaint is not entirely true: Venutius, the former husband of Cartimandua who had earlier tried to stir up a rebellion against her (see n. 49 above), now tried again with greater success (Tac. *Hist.* 3.45); Bolanus managed to rescue Cartimandua, although not to oust Venutius, and archaeological evidence suggests that he may have made considerable inroads into Brigantian territory and even beyond (see also Statius, *Silvae* 5.2.142–9). It was under Bolanus' command in 70 that Agricola arrived to take command of Legio XX Valeria (*Agr.* 7–8).

60. *Petilius Cerialis*: Governor 71–3 (the name is spelt 'Petillius' in inscriptions); he had previously been legate of Legio IX Hispana during the revolt of Boudicca (Tac. *Ann.* 14.32.3), and is thus the first governor of Britannia known to have had previous

experience there. Immediately prior to his appointment in Britannia he had played a key role in putting down the revolt of Civilis in the Rhineland (see Introduction A5), and so may have been seen by Vespasian as something of a trouble-shooter for areas of discontent.

61. *a great part of their territory*: The territory of the Brigantes apparently extended from Yorkshire up to the Tyne–Solway line. For their earlier relations with Rome, see nn. 46, 49 and 59 above. Cerialis is generally thought to have relocated Legio IX Hispana from Lindum (mod. Lincoln) to Eburacum (mod. York) and to have penetrated into the northern Pennines and perhaps even into southern Scotland; archaeological evidence shows that the first Roman fort at Luguvalium (mod. Carlisle) dates to his governorship.

62. *Julius Frontinus*: Governor 74–7; although Frontius was one of the most important men of his day, and the author of still-extant works on aqueducts and military strategy, Tacitus' brief comments here are all that is known of his governorship of Britannia; he was probably active in northern England as well as Wales, and may have been responsible for the construction of a new legionary fortress at Deva (mod. Chester).

63. *swimming with arms and horses under control*: The auxiliaries in question were probably Batavi, since Tacitus later says that some were serving under Agricola (*Agr.* 36 with n. 88) and they were recognized as having special skill in this sort of swimming (Tac. *Hist.* 4.12.3, *Ann.* 2.8.3; Dio 69.9.6; *ILS* 2558); see further *Germ.* 29 with nn. 77 and 78.

64. *the tax itself*: Tacitus seems to describe two schemes here. First, provincials who did not have enough grain of their own to meet the requisition would be forced to buy from the imperial granaries at a fixed price, simply in order to sell it back at a lower price; secondly, they might be ordered to deliver it to an inaccessible location, and would then resort to bribes in order to be excused.

65. *garrisons and forts*: Tacitus provides no indication of where these actions took place; it was presumably northern England or southern Scotland.

66. *temples … proper houses*: Structures typical of Roman-style settlements; the Britanni of course already had houses, but Tacitus means houses of the Roman type. A fragmentary inscription from Verulamium records the dedication of an unidentifiable public building in 79, during Agricola's governorship (*AE* 1957, no. 169).

67. *liberal arts*: We know by chance of one man who probably played a role in Agricola's programme of education. Two Greek inscriptions found at York record dedications (one to 'the gods of the governor's headquarters') made by a certain Scribonius Demetrius (*RIB* 1.662–3); this is almost certainly the scholar Demetrius of Tarsus, a major character in Plutarch's dialogue *On the Obsolescence of Oracles*, who is said there to be on his way home from Britannia (410a) and who describes his visit to outlying islands inhabited only by holy men (419e–420a).

68. *passion to command it*: This development later received the satirical attention of Juvenal, writing probably in the late 120s: 'eloquent Gaul has taught the Britanni to plead court cases, and Thule now talks about hiring a teacher of rhetoric' (15.111–12).

69. *The third year ... was ravaged*: 'Taus' is the Latin name for the Tay. It was as a result of Agricola's successes in this year that Titus received his fifteenth acclamation as *imperator* (Dio 66.20.3).

70. *within Britannia itself*: Tacitus' awkward language here has suggested to some scholars that Titus, who had become emperor the year before, had indeed decided to establish a frontier here, and that Domitian, whose name Tacitus suppresses, reversed this decision and authorized the advance into Caledonia. The Forth–Clyde isthmus was later the site for the wall of Antoninus Pius, but archaeological evidence for border defences of Agricolan date is scanty; a line of frontier forts extending up to Perth, however, may date to this period.

71. *nations hitherto unknown*: The lack of detail in Tacitus' account has led to much discussion of what sea and what nations are meant here; there is some consensus that the sea is the Firth of Clyde and that the nations were in what is now Ayrshire and/or Galloway; if so, Tacitus in the previous chapter must have exaggerated the extent to which territory south of the Forth–Clyde isthmus had already been pacified.

72. *between Britannia and Hispania*: For the misconception that the west coast of Britannia faced Hispania, see *Agr.* 10 with n. 26.

73. *beyond the Bodotria*: That is, the Firth of Forth; Tacitus' lack of further geographical detail makes it impossible to know how far north Agricola pushed during this campaign, but some scholars argue that he advanced as far as the Moray Firth. A number of Roman camps have been identified in this area, one as far north as the mouth of the Spey, but dating is uncertain; even those that are definitely of Flavian date may have been constructed under Agricola's successor. Construction of the legionary fortress at

Inchtuthil (on the banks of the Tay some 15 miles north of Perth) is often attributed to Agricola, but the fact that it was still incomplete when it was abandoned in 86 or 87 suggests that it may have been begun after Agricola had already left the province.

74. *Usipi*: A Germanic people; see further *Germ.* 32 with n. 83.

75. *deserve record*: This episode was long remembered, since it was also recorded by Dio over a century later (66.20.1–2); some scholars have also thought that it featured in a now lost epic poem by a certain Pompullus, mocked by Martial in a poem of *c.* 90 (*Epigrams* 6.61). Tacitus here uses it as a digression to mark off the short accounts of Agricola's first six years in Britannia from the more detailed narrative that follows.

76. *three Liburnians*: 'Liburnian' was a term loosely applied to small fast-sailing warships, usually with two banks of oars, that were apparently first used by the Liburni, a people on the north coast of the Adriatic.

77. *Suebi … Frisii*: Two Germanic peoples. 'Suebi' was a term used in several different senses by Roman writers; see further *Germ.* 38 with n. 107. Here Tacitus is apparently applying it to some coastal people. The Frisii lived on the coast of what is now the eastern Netherlands; see further *Germ.* 34 with n. 90.

78. *born the year before*: We may infer from this that Agricola's wife, Domitia Decidiana, accompanied him during his governorship of Britannia. The Vindolanda tablets suggest that this was normal for the wives of officers; see especially *TV* 2.291, a birthday invitation from one of these wives to another.

79. *Mons Graupius*: 'The Graupian Mountain'; the identification of this battle site has been the object of considerable investigation for many generations. Although a number of sites have been proposed, from south of the Tay to just east of the mouth of the Spey, none has ever won general acceptance. The name appeared as 'Grampius' in the first printed edition of *Agricola* (*c.* 1480), which led early Scottish antiquarians to rename the entire range as the Grampian Mountains.

80. *'old age was fresh and green'*: A quotation from Virgil, *Aeneid* 6.304.

81. *Calgacus*: The name is related to Irish *calgach* and means 'swordsman', but nothing more is known of the historical Calgacus. The speech that Tacitus presents here is his own carefully constructed composition; with its profusion of striking epigrams, it is very much in the style of the rhetorical exercises known as *declamationes*. The sentiments are typical of speeches

that Roman historians put in the mouths of resistance leaders;
see, for example, Caes. *Gall.* 7.77 and Sallust, *Histories* 4.67.

82. *The Brigantes*: Evidently a slip on Tacitus' part; the revolt to
which he refers is that of the Iceni under Boudicca in 60 (see *Agr.*
16 with n. 54), in which the Brigantes are not known to have
played any part. The slip was perhaps due to the fact that the
Brigantes were also ruled by a woman, Cartimandua, although
she was a loyal ally of Rome.

83. *are fighting ... after second thoughts*: There is a problem with
the Latin text here that has not been satisfactorily resolved, but the
general sense must be along the lines given here.

84. *agglomeration of nations*: The reference here is to the numerous
auxiliaries that served in the Roman army; Tacitus has already
mentioned a cohort of Germanic Usipi (*Agr.* 28 with n. 74) and
below mentions cohorts of Tungri and Batavi (*Agr.* 36 with n. 88).
Britannic cavalry are attested in the Roman army as early as 69
(Tac. *Hist.* 3.41.1), and infantry cohorts of Britanni begin to appear
in Roman military documents by 80.

85. *addressed them thus*: Although Tacitus may well have heard an
account of Agricola's speech, what he presents here is again most
likely to be his own composition. Hortatory speeches delivered
by generals before battles were a staple of Roman historiography, sometimes presented as here in pairs; see, for example,
Livy 21.40–44.

86. *come to grips*: There is again a problem with the Latin text here,
but the general sense is likely to be as given.

87. *charioteers*: The term Tacitus uses here is *covinnarius eques*, literally 'the *covinnus*-cavalry'. The term *covinnus* was Celtic in
origin (cf. Old Irish *fen*, Welsh *gwain*, 'wagon'), and was used by
Latin writers to denote the war-chariot of the Britanni and the
northern Gauls; according to Mela (3.52), they had scythes
attaches to the axles.

88. *Batavi ... Tungri*: Two Germanic peoples; for the Batavi, see
further *Germ.* 29 with nn. 77–8; for the Tungri, *Germ.* 2 with
n. 8. Cohorts of Batavi and Tungri are well attested in Britannia:
the Vindolanda tablets indicate that the garrison there for the
period *c.* 92–103 included the First Cohort of Tungri (see
especially *TV* 2.154, a strength report on the unit), the Ninth
Cohort of Batavi and possibly the Third Cohort of Batavi
as well, and inscriptions found elsewhere along Hadrian's
Wall provide evidence for the First Cohort of Batavi (*ILS*
2549) and the Second Cohort of Tungri (*ILS* 2554); it is likely

that some of these were among the cohorts that served under Agricola.

89. *Boresti*: Nothing else is known of this people or of their location, and there may be a problem with the text.

90. *Trucculum*: Nothing else is known of this port or of its location; there are also problems with the Latin in the last part of the sentence. Most scholars agree that the text is probably corrupt, but none of the numerous attempts to emend it has gained wide acceptance.

91. *sham triumph over Germania*: Domitian celebrated a triumph over the Germanic Chatti in probably the late summer of 83. At *Germ.* 37, Tacitus again refers to this triumph in disparaging terms, and the younger Pliny (*Pan.* 16.3) also seems to allude to the story about the sham prisoners of war; it was clearly widespread. Yet it may not have been true; it is worth noting that a very similar story was told about the emperor Gaius (Suet. *Calig.* 47).

92. *intended for Agricola*: Syria, like Britannia, was governed by legates of the emperor, who could therefore appoint and dismiss them at will. T. Atilius Rufus had been governor of Pannonia in 80 (*CIL* XVI.26) and is attested in Syria by a milestone dating to 83 (*AE* 1925, no. 95).

93. *successor*: Agricola's successor in Britannia is unknown; the only other governor of Britannia attested for the reign of Domitian is Sallustius Lucullus, known from a very brief mention in Suetonius (*Dom.* 10.3).

94. *One after another ... all those cohorts*: Tacitus here alludes to a series of military defeats that took place in Europe from the mid 80s to the early 90s. The details of these are uncertain, since the sources are extremely meagre: a short notice in Suetonius (*Dom.* 6.1), some erratic summaries of Dio's history (67.6–7 and 10) and a few inscriptions and brief allusions. The generally accepted reconstruction is that in 85 the Dacians, under their king Decebalus, crossed into Moesia and defeated the Roman governor there. Domitian drove them back, but after his departure his general Cornelius Fuscus, whom Tacitus elsewhere describes as something of a daredevil (*Hist.* 2.86.3), invaded Dacia, was defeated and killed. In 89 Domitian attacked the Germanic Marcomani for not aiding him against the Dacians, but was defeated by them and their allies the Iazyges. Lastly, in 92, the Iazyges invaded Pannonia and destroyed a legion. During this period there were also Roman victories, for which Domitian celebrated additional triumphs, but Tacitus does not mention these.

95. *riverbank*: That is, the Danube as the frontier of the empire; see *Germ.* 1 with n. 1.

96. *the proconsulship of Africa or Asia*: The two most important provinces governed by proconsuls rather than legates of the emperors. The positions were awarded by lot to the two most senior consulars who had not previously held either; known instances in this period suggest that Agricola's turn would have come some twelve to fifteen years after his consulship, thus dating this episode to *c.* 90.

97. *execution of Civica still fresh in memory*: C. Vettulenus Civica Cerialis had been the legate of Moesia in 82 (*ILS* 1995) and was put to death by Domitian while serving as proconsul of Asia (Suet. *Dom.* 10.2), probably in 87 or 88.

98. *ostentatious death*: Tacitus here seems to have in mind the fatal opposition of men like Thrasea Paetus under Nero, Helvidius Priscus under Vespasian and, most immediately, Herennius Senecio, Arulenus Rusticus and the younger Helvidius under Domitian; see further *Agr.* 2 with n. 3, *Agr.* 45 with nn. 103–5, and Introduction C2.

99. *that he had been poisoned*: Dio (66.20.3) states as a bald fact that Agricola 'was murdered by Domitian'. Rumours of poisoning were common in antiquity, when a lack of medical knowledge meant that sudden and unexpectedly fatal illnesses could easily be blamed on human intervention. Although in this passage Tacitus is carefully non-committal, his language in the remainder of the work repeatedly suggests that he believed the rumour to be true.

100. *no emperor but a bad one*: Under Augustus it became common to leave a bequest to the emperor as a mark of esteem (Suet. *Aug.* 66.4); although Augustus himself was said to have handed over all such bequests to the deceased's children, it was a conventional charge against bad emperors that they not only accepted them but manipulated the practice in order to maximize their take (Suet. *Calig.* 38.2, *Nero* 32.2). Domitian was said at first to have refused these inheritances, but later to have sought them out (Suet. *Dom.* 9.2, 12.2).

101. *Agricola was born ... Priscinus*: That is, he was born on 13 June 40 and died 23 August 93. Gaius alone is named as consul for the year 40 because his intended colleague died before the beginning of the year (Suet. *Calig.* 17.1, Dio 59.24.2).

102. *principate of Trajan*: The lack here of any reference to Nerva (contrast *Agr.* 3) suggests that this passage was written after Nerva's death on 27 January 98.

103. *so many consulars ... exile and flight*: Tacitus refers here to the
trials of 93; see Introduction C2, and *Agr.* 2 with n. 3, as well as
the following two notes. The younger Pliny (*Ep.* 3.11.3) provides
a list of victims: 'Senecio, Rusticus and Helvidius killed; Mauricus,
Gratilla, Arria and Fannia exiled.' Of these, Rusticus and Helvidius
were consulars; Herennius Senecio had refused to hold any position
higher than that of quaestor (Dio 67.13.2). Mauricus was Rusticus'
brother, and Gratilla was apparently his wife (Plin. *Ep.* 5.1.8);
Arria was the widow of Thrasea Paetus; Fannia was their daughter
as well as the widow of Helvidius Priscus. Fannia's condemnation
was apparently due to the aid she gave to Herennius Senecio in his
laudatory account of her husband's death (Plin. *Ep.* 7.19.5). The
exiles returned early in 97 (Plin. *Ep.* 1.5.16, 9.13.5), not long before
Tacitus began work on *Agricola*.

104. *Carus Mettius ... in the dock*: Mettius Carus played a leading
role in the prosecutions of Herennius Senecio and Fannia (Plin.
Ep. 1.5.3, 7.19.5); successful prosecutions of this sort are what
Tacitus means by 'victories'. The senator L. Valerius Catullus
Messalinus was notorious for his bloodthirsty advice to Domitian
(Plin. *Ep.* 4.22.5; cf. Juv. 4.113); the 'Alban fortress' is the great
villa that Domitian built in the Alban Hills outside Rome. Baebius
Massa, having been charged with extortion during his proconsulship, was prosecuted jointly by Herennius Senecio and the
younger Pliny and convicted (Plin. *Ep.* 7.33.4–8; cf. 3.4.4 and
6.29.8); it is presumably to this trial that Tacitus refers.

105. *Helvidius ... guiltless blood*: This Helvidius was the son of the
Helvidius Priscus mentioned in *Agr.* 2; he was executed for an
alleged allusion to Domitian in a farce that he wrote (Suet. *Dom.*
10.4). For Arulenus Rusticus and Herennius Senecio, see *Agr.* 2
with n. 3; for Mauricus, see n. 103 above.

106. *four years before he died*: Tacitus was presumably absent from
Rome in some official capacity, probably as the commander of a
legion; see Introduction B1.

Notes to *Germania*

1. *by the Rhine and Danube rivers*: These rivers were conventionally regarded as the boundaries of Roman rule in Europe, even
though as Tacitus notes below (*Germ.* 29) in some places it
extended beyond them.

2. *Sarmatians and Dacians*: Peoples north of the Danube. 'Sarmatian'
was a collective term for a number of nomadic peoples in eastern

Europe and southern Russia; Tacitus probably had in mind the Iazyges of the Hungarian plain, with whom Domitian had been at war in 92. The Dacians were a people in what is now Romania; under their king Decebalus, they had crossed the Danube and attacked the province of Moesia in 85, sparking a series of wars that lasted into the late 80s, when Domitian made peace with Decebalus and recognized his rule. Shortly after Tacitus wrote *Germania*, however, war broke out again, ending with Trajan's incorporation of Dacia into the empire. See further *Agr.* 41 with n. 94.

3. *nations and kings unknown before*: In the northern seas; the 'broad promontories' must refer particularly to Jutland and the 'vast islands' probably include southern Scandinavia, thought to be an island in antiquity (see n. 128 below). Since the last Roman military activity in this region took place in the late teens AD, Tacitus must be using the phrase 'recent times' rather loosely.

4. *Tuisto*: There is no other evidence for this figure, although the name seems to derive from a Germanic root meaning 'double' or 'twofold' (as in 'twist' and 'twin'), and may mean 'hermaphrodite' (like modern German *Zwitter*). Some scholars compare the primordial giant Ymir, mentioned several times in the collection of Old Norse mythological poetry known as the Poetic Edda.

5. *Mannus*: There is again no other evidence for this figure, although the name is clearly connected with the Germanic word for 'man'.

6. *Ingvaeones ... Istvaeones*: The same set of names appears in the elder Pliny (*NH* 4.99–100), who presents them as groupings of several peoples: the Ingvaeones include the Cimbri, Teutones and Chauci, and the Herminones include the Suebi, Hermunduri, Chatti and Cherusci; a problem with the manuscript makes it uncertain which peoples he assigned to the Istvaeones. The spelling of the names is uncertain; I have here used the forms that seem most likely on etymological grounds: 'Ingvaeones' seems connected to the later Scandinavian divine name 'Yngvi', and 'Herminones' probably derives from the reconstructed Germanic root *ermin-*, meaning 'great, powerful'.

7. *Marsi ... Vandilii*: Tacitus mentions the Marsi several times in connection with the campaigns of Germanicus in 14–16 (*Ann.* 1.50.4 and 56.5, 2.25.1; cf. Strabo 7.1.3). The only other author to mention the Gambrivii is Strabo (7.1.3); their name seems related to that of the Sugambri, an important people in the time of Augustus. For the Suebi, see *Germ.* 38 with n. 107. According to Pliny (*NH* 4.99), the 'Vandili' were another grouping of

several peoples, the Burgodiones, Varinnae, Charini and Gutones; the name does not otherwise occur until much later.

8.   *then called Germani*: There are some problems with the text in this sentence, but the meaning is probably close to the translation given here. The Tungri were a people of northeastern Gaul, centred on what is now the town of Tongeren in Belgium; they are first mentioned by the elder Pliny (*NH* 4.106), and cohorts of Tungri are attested as serving in the Roman army in Britannia from late first to the mid second century (see *Agr.* 36 with n. 88). There is no other evidence that they were the first Germanic people to cross the Rhine into Gaul or ever had the particular name 'Germani'. Caesar, however, refers to a group of peoples west of the Rhine who were collectively known as 'Germani' (*Gall.* 2.4.10; cf. 6.32.1), and some scholars think that the Tungri may have been a later regrouping of those peoples.

9.   *adopted it themselves*: There are textual problems with this sentence as well, and its meaning has been much debated; the translation offered here reflects a common interpretation. There is in fact no evidence that the peoples whom the Romans called Germani ever used that name for themselves except in Roman contexts.

10. *Hercules ... on their way into battle*: This is presumably an instance of *interpretatio Romana* (see *Germ.* 43 with n. 125), in which an interpreter identified a Germanic warrior hero with the Graeco-Roman hero Hercules.

11. *barritus, they call it*: The majority of manuscripts read *barditus*, but many editors prefer this emendation, based on a passage of the late fourth-century historian Ammianus Marcellinus (16.12.43; cf. 26.7.17); he describes how a Germanic army 'raised as great a *barritus* as possible: this shout, rising from a spare rumble and gradually growing, has the effect of waves flung against the cliffs'.

12. *Asciburgium ... inhabited today*: The Peutinger Table, a medieval copy of a late Roman road map, locates this town on the Rhine opposite the confluence of the Ruhr; Tacitus elsewhere (*Hist.* 4.33.1) mentions it as the base of a cavalry unit in 70. Its connection with Ulysses was presumably due to a false derivation of the name from the Greek words *askos*, 'skin bag', and *purgos*, 'fort', referring to the bag of winds given to him by the wind-god Aeolus (Homer, *Odyssey* 10.1–79); many manuscripts actually add the name in Greek script, 'Askipurgion', but this is probably a later insertion. The name more likely derives from the

Germanic words for 'ash-tree' and 'mountain' (cf. modern German *Esche* and *Berg*).

13. *monuments ... on the borders of Germania and Raetia*: That is, roughly modern Bavaria. The Gauls are known to have used the Greek alphabet (Caes. *Gall.* 6.14.3), and a number of Gallo-Greek inscriptions have been found in what is now Provence. If Caesar is right in claiming that the Helvetii in what is now Switzerland also used Greek (*Gall.* 1.29.1), it is not impossible that people further to the east did as well.

14. *unique of its kind*: Despite this assertion, the physical traits that Tacitus attributes to the Germani are all commonplaces of Greek and Roman descriptions of various northern peoples, especially the Gauls; see, for example, Diod. Sic. 5.28.1 and Livy 38.17.3.

15. *violent effort ... cold and hunger*: More commonplaces. Compare these remarks of Livy about the Gauls: 'a race to whom nature has given bodies and spirits more big than enduring' (5.44.4), 'all of whose force lies in the attack' (7.12.11); they have 'bodies completely unable to bear labour and heat' (10.28.4), but are 'a race accustomed to cold and damp' (5.48.3).

16. *grain crops ... fruit trees*: Excavations from the coastal regions of the Netherlands, northern Germany and Denmark have revealed considerable cultivation of grains, especially wheat and barley. The 'fruit trees' that Tacitus had in mind may have been in particular the olive and the grape, staples of the Mediterranean diet.

17. *form of wealth*: Excavations confirm the importance of cattle, the remains of which typically account for over half the animal bones at Germanic settlements. Study of these remains indicates that Germanic cattle were indeed smaller than those in the Mediterranean, where selective breeding had been practised for many generations.

18. *as lightly esteemed as earthenware*: A familiar image of philosophic disdain for wealth (see Seneca, *Epistles* 5.6). In fact, high-quality Roman silverware has been found throughout Germanic territory in carefully buried hoards, suggesting that Tacitus was here simply relying on ethnographic commonplaces about 'barbarian' indifference to wealth.

19. *denarii ... common goods*: The denarius was a silver coin first minted in Rome in the late third century BC; denarii with notched edges were among the first produced, and lasted down to the 60s BC, while those depicting a chariot date from the 170s to the 40s BC. The evidence of coin hoards does suggest a preference for

older coins, although some scholars have argued that this simply reflects the volume of coins in distribution; the preference for silver coins over gold, however, is clear.

20. *character of their weapons*: Although Tacitus is wrong about supplies of iron, which was in fact fairly abundant in Germanic regions, his account of their weapons matches reasonably well with the results of archaeological excavations; these show that light lances and spears were the chief offensive weapon, with light shields the only form of defensive gear. Swords were also used, but appear less frequently, and breastplates and helmets were effectively unknown.

21. *mixed groups*: Caesar provides a more detailed description of the Germanic practice of combining cavalry and infantry (*Gall.* 1.48.5–7); it was a practice that he admired enough to adopt himself (*Civ.* 3.75.5 and 84.3).

22. *not absolute or arbitrary*: In Roman thought, regal power was by definition absolute, and so Tacitus' observation here is a strong statement of the Germanic devotion to freedom; see Introduction D2.

23. *taken from their sacred groves*: Presumably not images of the gods, but rather 'the images of wild beasts brought from woods and groves' that Tacitus mentions elsewhere (*Hist.* 4.22.2); see further *Germ.* 9.

24. *holy and prophetic*: For other references to the importance of women as diviners among the Germani, see Caes. *Gall.* 1.50.4–5, Strabo 7.2.3, Suet. *Vit.* 14.5 and Dio 67.5.3; perhaps most intriguing is a list of military officers and servants from a Roman camp in Egypt, dating to the second century, that includes 'Baloubourg, the sibyl of the Semnones' (*Sammelbuch griechischer Urkunden aus Ägypten*, vol. 3, F. Bilabel, ed. (Berlin and Leipzig: 1926), no. 6221).

25. *as a divinity*: According to Tacitus (*Hist.* 4.61.2 and 65.3–4, 5.22.3 and 24.1), this woman held considerable authority among the peoples involved in the revolt of Civilis (see Introduction A5) because 'she had foretold success for the Germani and the destruction of the legions'; both the Germani and the Romans evidently regarded her as important as Civilis himself. A brief reference in a poem of Statius (*Silvae* 1.4.90) indicates that she was captured in 77 or 78 and taken to Rome, and a fragmentary inscription from the Italian town of Ardea contains a Greek poem about her, although its interpretation is disputed (*AE* 1953, no. 25 = *AE* 1955, no. 75).

26. *Aurinia*: Nothing else is known of this woman; some scholars have suggested that the name should be emended to Albruna, meaning something like 'the trusted friend of the elves'.

27. *turning women into goddesses*: A pointed reference to the Roman practice of deifying female members of the imperial family.

28. *As for the gods ... normally allowed*: Tacitus follows normal practice in referring to Germanic gods by their Roman equivalents (see *Germ.* 43 with n. 125). The three deities he names regularly appear in inscriptions from the area of the lower Rhine, in some cases with obviously Germanic epithets (e.g., Mercury Hranno, Hercules Magusanus, Mars Halamarthus). We should perhaps identify Mercury with Woden/Odin, Hercules (presumably distinct from the Hercules mentioned in *Germ.* 3) with Donar/Thor and Mars with Tiw/Tyr, although such equivalences were complex and shifting. It was a commonplace of Graeco-Roman ethnography to attribute human sacrifice to foreigners and barbarians, although archaeological findings suggest that the ancient Germanic peoples did sometimes engage in it.

29. *Isis ... from abroad*: The cult of the Egyptian goddess Isis was by Tacitus' day widely spread throughout the area of the Roman empire, and is solidly if not abundantly attested in the provinces that bordered Germania. But since it seems to have spread with Graeco-Roman culture, most scholars believe that Tacitus has misidentified a native Germanic ritual that bore some resemblance to a well-known Isiac ritual that involved a ship (see Apuleius, *Metamorphoses* 11.16). For the Liburnian, see *Agr.* 28 with n. 76.

30. *only by the eye of reverence*: Since it was the norm among Greeks and Romans to depict the gods in human form and dedicate temples to them, they took particular note when other peoples did not observe these customs; they also tended to attribute to them explanations that may reflect Graeco-Roman philosophical debates more than native beliefs. Tacitus is probably right about the absence of Germanic temples and divine images, although the evidence is sparse and difficult to assess; for other references to sacred groves, see *Germ.* 7, 10, 39, 40, 43; *Ann.* 1.61.3, 2.12.1, 4.73.4; *Hist.* 4.14.2.

31. *casting lots*: A common form of divination, found among many peoples and attested among the Germani also by Caesar (*Gall.* 1.53.7). It is not impossible that the signs with which the strips were marked were actually runes, since the earliest known runic inscriptions date to the early third century.

32. *warnings from horses*: Divination from birds was highly developed
    in Rome in the form of augury, but the use of horses was more
    unusual; the cultic importance of horses in Germanic culture is
    well attested.

33. *by nights*: The practice of reckoning the new day from sunset
    rather than sunrise occurs in many cultures (for example, in the
    Jewish and Muslim calendars), and according to Caesar was
    observed by the Gauls (*Gall.* 6.18.2). Among Germanic peoples,
    the Anglo-Saxons are known to have defined periods of time by
    the number of nights, a usage that survives in the term 'fort-
    night', an abbreviation of 'fourteen nights'.

34. *clash their spears*: Both Caesar (*Gall.* 7.21.1) and Tacitus else-
    where (*Hist.* 5.17.3) describe Gauls showing their approval by
    making a noise with their weapons.

35. *cowardly ... cover of wicker*: Comparison with Tacitus' other
    writings suggests that by 'those who disgrace their bodies' he had
    in mind effeminate men who took a passive role in sex with other
    men. Hundreds of human bodies have been recovered from bogs,
    preserved by the acidic action of peat, dating as far back as the
    early Iron Age. Although these so-called 'bog bodies' vary widely
    in circumstances and age, some of them provide corroboration
    for the general use of bogs as sites of ritualized killing and for the
    particular practice of weighing down bodies.

36. *horses or cattle*: There is ample evidence in early medieval Ger-
    manic law for the practice of compensating injured parties by the
    payment of fines, and even for the payment of part of the fine to
    the king or court. Several codes include extensive schedules of
    payments, calibrated to the nature of the injury; although the
    fines are expressed in monetary sums, at least one code provides
    a list of equivalencies between coins and livestock.

37. *except under arms*: The point of this comment is that the Romans
    traditionally made a strict distinction between the military sphere,
    in which men routinely bore arms, and the civil sphere, in
    which they did not; the observation that the Germani always
    bore arms was a sign of their barbarous and warlike nature (cf.
    Livy 21.20.1 on the Gauls). The comment that follows makes the
    same point: whereas Roman boys marked their coming of age by
    donning a toga, the symbol of civil life, Germanic boys are given
    weapons.

38. *ranks of the companions*: Scholars have long debated the precise
    meaning of the Latin in this and the preceding sentence, without
    reaching any consensus. In the first sentence, the phrase *dignatio*

principis can mean either 'the rank of leader', as translated here, or 'the recognition of a leader'; both are possible, although the former is more in keeping with Tacitus' normal usage. In the second sentence, I have accepted the emendation of *ceteri* for the manuscript reading *ceteris*, and have translated accordingly; the manuscript reading would translate as 'they [i.e., the 'mere lads' of the previous sentence] are attached to the others who are more mature and approved'.

39. *This order ... reputation*: Many scholars have regarded Tacitus' account of this 'order of companions' (Latin *comitatus*) in this and the following chapters as the earliest description of a distinctively Germanic social institution: an all-male group consisting of a leader and his followers bound together by mutual obligations. Such warrior bands certainly existed, among the Gauls as well as the Germani (e.g., Caes. *Gall*. 3.22.1–3, 6.15; Tac. *Ann*. 1.57.3, 2.45.1). Tacitus' account here, however, contains a number of commonplaces, and he has clearly shaped it to suit the overall image of the Germani that he wants to create (see Introduction D2); it would thus be rash to take it at face value.

40. *To outlive ... shame*: Several Roman writers attribute to the Gauls the custom that a leader's followers should not outlive him (e.g., Caes. *Gall*. 3.22.1–3), but only a single late source (Ammianus Marcellinus, *History* 16.12.60) attributes it to the Germani.

41. *buy with blood*: A pointed contrast to the Roman ideal of the farmer-soldier, who used the same qualities of discipline and steadfast labour to conquer both his enemies and the earth; these are virtues that the Germani, for all their ferocity, lack.

42. *metal discs and collars*: These are standard Roman military decorations, but few examples have been found in Germanic areas that date to the time of Tacitus.

43. *houses set close together*: Tacitus' account of Germanic building practices fits fairly well with the archaeological evidence. Villages seem to have been relatively common, ranging from small hamlets of three or four houses to organized communities of twelve to eighteen houses; the houses are always spaced apart, however, and often have fenced areas around them. The use of stone and brick seems to have been unknown, but woodworking was highly developed; Tacitus' dismissive comment simply reflects a cultural prejudice against timber construction. Only the underground pits that he describes at the end of this chapter have no match in the archaeological record.

44. *short cloak*: The Latin word is *sagum*. Both the word and the garment were Gallic in origin; many ancient writers treat the *sagum* as the typical garment of the Gauls (e.g., Diod. Sic. 5.30.1, Strabo 4.4.3). Large rectangular textiles corresponding closely to what ancient writers say about the *sagum* have been discovered in north European bogs, providing some confirmation for Tacitus' statement that the garment was in common use among the Germani as well.

45. *clothing ... every limb*: The reference to the Sarmatians (*Germ.* 1 with n. 2) and Parthians (*Germ.* 37 with n. 98) indicates that by 'clothing' Tacitus had in mind here trousers and long-sleeved tunics, garments closely associated with those peoples; along with the *sagum*, trousers were also regarded as a garment typical of the Gauls (Diod. Sic. 5.30.1, Strabo 4.4.3). Roman reliefs and statuettes frequently depict Germani with trousers and long-sleeved tunics, and actual examples have been recovered from bogs.

46. *pelts of wild animals*: It was conventional in descriptions of Germani from Caesar onwards to refer to clothing made from the skins of wild animals (Caes. *Gall.* 4.1.10, 6.21.5; Tac. *Hist.* 2.88.3); although these descriptions presumably had some basis in fact, they were probably shaped more by a desire to stress their lack of civilization than by actual observations. Examples of skin capes have in fact been found in bogs, but the skins are mostly those of sheep, sometimes of cattle.

47. *dress of the women ... upper arms bare*: This description conforms closely to the depiction of Germanic women in Roman art, and also fits two long garments found in Danish bogs. Linen had been produced in Europe for centuries, and the elder Pliny comments on its popularity among Germanic women (*NH* 19.8–9). In the Mediterranean world, most purple dye came from various species of shellfish; the purple referred to here is more likely to have been the indigo that comes from woad, a dye found in a number of ancient textiles from Scandinavia.

48. *oxen ... sword*: The custom to which Tacitus refers was presumably what anthropologists call a bride-price, in which the groom's family gives a gift to the bride's family in exchange for the bride; the custom continued among Germanic peoples well into the early Middle Ages. Tacitus interprets it in terms of the normal Roman practice of dowry, property that the bride brought to the marriage and over which she and her family retained certain rights.

49. *immune from the hazards of war*: See *Germ.* 7–8. Tacitus' interpretation of these Germanic customs is almost certainly his own, meant to emphasize once again the central role of warfare in Germanic life.

50. *good laws are elsewhere*: A commonplace of Roman moralizing (cf. Horace, *Odes* 3.24.35–6). Throughout this entire discussion the implied contrast between the morality of the barbarian Germani and the corruption of the civilized Romans is particularly clear, and is emphasized by Tacitus' highly rhetorical language; see Introduction D2.

51. *maids and nurses*: The use of wet-nurses was common among the upper classes of Rome in Tacitus' day, and the breast-feeding of children by their own mother was considered one of the markers of the good old days (Tac. *Dial.* 28.4 and 29.1; Aulus Gellius, *Attic Nights* 12.1).

52. *young men ... marriage*: Both Caesar (*Gall.* 6.21.4–5) and Mela (3.26) note that the Germani married late, at least by Roman standards; in the Roman world, it seems to have been normal for women to be in their late teens and men in their late twenties or early thirties at the time of their first marriage.

53. *no reward*: A dig at the much satirized Roman practice of legacy hunting, in which people would shower favours upon the childless wealthy in the hopes that they would make them their heirs (e.g., Horace, *Satires* 2.5; Petronius, *Satyricon* 116; Juv. 12.93–130).

54. *receives satisfaction*: Hereditary feuds are well attested among Germanic peoples during the Middle Ages, and Tacitus' description here fits very well with the later evidence. For the system of payments, see *Germ.* 12 with n. 36; the best known of these was the wergeld, payments exacted for manslaughter that varied according to the status, age and sex of the victim.

55. *turn ... from your door*: Caesar makes a very similar observation (*Gall.* 6.23.9); this emphasis on private hospitality is typical of archaic societies in which there were few public institutions for the protection and support of travellers.

56. *There is ... host and guest*: Many editors regard this sentence, which is not only redundant but constitutes a very flat ending for this discussion, as a marginal note by a scholar that a later copyist mistakenly incorporated into the text.

57. *a table for each*: The point of this observation is the implicit contrast with Graeco-Roman practice, in which diners shared couches and used a common table.

58. *neither canny nor cunning*: It was a stereotype of Graeco-Roman
     ethnography that northern peoples were courageous but dim,
     southern peoples quick-witted but cowardly; see Introduction
     D1. In fact, Roman writers often complained about what they
     perceived as Germanic deceitfulness and treachery (Caes. *Gall.*
     1.40.8, 4.13.1 and 4); the historian Velleius Paterculus, who
     fought against the Germani under Tiberius, characterizes them
     as 'a race born to deceit' (2.118.1).

59. *they debate ... mistake*: Herodotus says almost exactly the same
     thing about the Persians: they deliberate about important mat-
     ters when drunk, and then reconsider their decision the next day
     (*Histories* 1.133.3–4); it is very likely that this became an ethno-
     graphic commonplace that was eventually attached to the
     Germani.

60. *something like wine*: Beer, obviously, with which the Romans
     were perfectly familiar even though they did not drink it them-
     selves. The elder Pliny lists a number of drinks made from grain:
     '*zythum* in Egypt, *caelia* and *cerea* in Hispania, *cervesia* and
     many other kinds in Gaul and other provinces' (*NH* 22.164).
     Cervesa was a common provision among the Tungrian and
     Batavian troops stationed at Vindolanda (*TV* 2.186 and 190),
     and a set of accounts there shows payments to a local brewer or
     cervesarius (*TV* 2.182.14); one squadron officer wrote to the
     commander of his cohort to say that 'my fellow soldiers have no
     beer; please order some to be sent' (*TV* 3.628). Brewers appear
     also in inscriptions from the Rhine frontier.

61. *wild fruit ... curdled milk*: This account of the Germanic diet
     does not fit well with Tacitus' earlier description of agriculture
     and animal husbandry (*Germ.* 5), but is very much in line with
     earlier accounts (Caes. *Gall.* 6.22.1, Strabo 7.1.3) that seem to
     have relied less on actual observation than on preconceived ideas
     about the Germani as nomads, for whom such a diet would be
     normal.

62. *dicing ... in their sober hours*: For the Romans, gambling at dice
     was a frivolous and not very respectable amusement, associated
     with after-dinner recreation and holidays. The interest of the
     Germani is borne out by the discovery of dice in Germanic graves
     of Tacitus' time.

63. *the slave obeys*: Tacitus' point of reference was the chattel slav-
     ery practised in Rome, in which slaves provided a vast range of
     services; the system he describes here seems to be something
     more like much later medieval serfdom.

64. *higher than free men or nobles*: There is no other evidence for the influence of royal freedmen among the Germani, and Tacitus' comment probably has less to do with conditions in Germania than in Rome (notoriously in the reign of Claudius: Suet. *Claud.* 25.5). Later Germanic tradition did, however, recognize statuses between slave and free, so that there may have been something like freedmen among the Germani of Tacitus' time.

65. *by whole villages*: This translates the Latin *ab universis vicis*, in which *vicis* is an emendation for the manuscript readings *vices*, 'changes', and *in vices*, 'in turn'; the former is unintelligible and the latter unsuited to Tacitus' style. Other emendations have also been proposed, but none has won general acceptance.

66. *ground to spare*: Tacitus seems to mean that every year a community takes possession of a certain amount of land, which it then divides among its members; the following year it moves on to fresh lands. Caesar says much the same thing, both about the Suebi (*Gall.* 4.1.7) and about the Germani in general (*Gall.* 6.22.2). All these accounts seem to derive from an a priori characterization of the Germani as nomadic rather than from actual observation of Germanic practice. Archaeological research shows that in fact the normal agricultural pattern in northern Europe during this time was one of fields with fixed boundaries that were worked over a number of years.

67. *alike unknown*: Despite this assertion, words for 'autumn' in later Germanic languages (Modern German *Herbst*, Old English *haerfest*, Old Norse *haust*) point to the existence of a common ancestor that probably dates back to the time of Tacitus.

68. *Divus Julius*: See Caes. *Gall.* 6.24.1: 'And there was in the past a time when the Gauls were superior to the Germani in valour, and on their own initiative brought war against them, and because of the size of the population and the scarcity of agricultural land sent colonies across the Rhine'; Tacitus also seems to have had this passage in mind at *Agr.* 11.

69. *crossed into Germania*: As discussed in the Introduction (A2), the idea of the Rhine as a clear-cut border between two distinct peoples owed more to Caesar's own agenda than to the cultural realities of the day.

70. *Hercynian Forest*: The name 'Hercynian' (or variations thereof) appears in Greek and Roman writers as early as the fourth century BC, but their remarks about its location are vague and sometimes at odds with each other. Some apparently used it as a general name for all the uplands of central Europe; Caesar, for

example, says that it extended from the Helvetii to the Dacians and took nine days to cross (*Gall.* 6.25). What Tacitus meant by it here is not at all clear, and not easily reconcilable with his later reference to it in connection with the Chatti in Hesse (*Germ.* 30).

71. *Helvetii were settled*: A Celtic people that in historical times lived in what is now western Switzerland; their attempt to migrate to land further west in 58 BC was the reason for Caesar's initial involvement in Gaul (*Gall.* 1.2–29), and in 15 BC their territory was incorporated into the empire; there is no other evidence that they had at one time lived further north near the Main.

72. *Boii ... change of inhabitants*: The Boii were also a Celtic people. Strabo locates them in the Hercynian Forest, apparently modern Bohemia, in the late second century BC (7.2.2; cf. 7.1.3); both he and Pliny also refer to the 'deserted lands of the Boii', which Pliny locates in what is now the border of Austria and Hungary (*NH* 3.146); some Boii accompanied the Helvetii in their attempted migration (Caes. *Gall.* 1.5.4 and 28.5). The name 'Boihaemum' (whence modern 'Bohemia') is clearly Germanic, from 'Boii' and the Germanic word for 'settlement' (cf. English 'ham', as in 'hamlet' and numerous place names).

73. *Aravisci ... Osi*: No other author mentions the latter, but the former appear under slightly different names in Pliny (*NH* 3.148) and in a number of inscriptions and coins; the personal names attested in the inscriptions seem to be Celtic rather than Pannonian. The description here of the Osi as a 'Germanic nation' is in flat contradiction to Tacitus' later assertion (*Germ.* 43) that they are not Germani; this may perhaps reflect a failure to reconcile conflicting sources, but it is more likely that, as many editors think, the phrase 'Germanic nation' originated as a marginal note by a later scholar that was mistakenly incorporated into the text.

74. *Treveri and Nervii*: Peoples of northeastern Gaul, both of whom were subdued by Caesar with some difficulty (*Gall.* 6.5–8 and 8.25 for the Treveri, 2.17–28 and 5.38–9 for the Nervii); both Caesar (*Gall.* 2.4.2) and Strabo (4.3.4) also refer to their supposed Germanic origin.

75. *Vangiones ... Nemetes*: Also described by Pliny as Germanic peoples living in Gaul (*NH* 4.106); the Vangiones lived around modern Worms, the Nemetes around Speyer, and the Triboci around Strasbourg (Ptol. 2.9.9).

76. *Ubii ... intruders*: The Ubii were the first people east of the Rhine to ally themselves with the Romans (Caes. *Gall.* 4.16.5); in the early 30s BC they were transferred at their own request to the Roman side of the river (Strabo 4.3.4) and settled in what is now Cologne. Agrippina, the daughter of Germanicus and wife of Claudius, was born there, and at her urging Claudius in 50 made the Ubian settlement a Roman colony (Tac. *Ann.* 12.27.1), with the official name Colonia Claudia Agrippinensis.

77. *island of the Rhine*: Formed by the split of the Rhine in what is now the Netherlands; it still carries the name Betuwe. Caesar refers in passing to 'the island of the Batavi' (*Gall.* 4.10.2), but says nothing else about them; they seem to have come to prominence during Augustus' attempted conquest of Germania, when they started serving as Roman auxiliaries (Dio 55.24.7, Tac. *Ann.* 2.8.3 and 11.1).

78. *'only to be used in war'*: There is no other evidence for the special privileges that Tacitus describes here, but the Batavi were certainly much used as auxiliaries. Batavian cohorts were stationed in Britannia from an early date and possibly took part in the conquest (*Agr.* 36 with n. 88); they are attested in other provinces as well. In addition, they served so frequently in the personal horse guards of the emperor that 'Batavi' came to be an informal name for those troops. The Batavi were especially known for their ability to swim across rivers with their arms and equipment (*Agr.* 18 with n. 63). Their revolt under Civilis in 69–70 (*Germ.* 37 with n. 105) does not seem to have adversely affected their status within the empire.

79. *Mattiaci*: A people living east of the Rhine, opposite modern Mainz; their capital was at the hot springs at Wiesbaden (Plin. *NH* 31.20); friendly relations with Rome began in the 40s (Tac. *Ann.* 11.20.3). During the Batavian revolt, they besieged the Roman legionary camp at Mainz (Tac. *Hist.* 4.37.3), after which the Romans increased their control over their territory; Domitian eventually incorporated it into his new province of Upper Germania.

80. *decumate lands*: The Latin term *agri decumates* appears in no other source, and the meaning of 'decumate', which is not a regular Latin word, is uncertain; it is often thought to be Celtic in origin, and related to the word for 'ten'. Many scholars think that the phrase meant something like 'the ten-canton lands'. They too were incorporated into Domitian's Upper Germania, so that Tacitus' dismissal of their inhabitants as genuine Germani

constitutes a subtle dig at Domitian's claims to victory over Germania; see Introduction D2.

81. *Chatti*: A people living in what is now the modern German state of Hesse (whose name seems to derive from that of the Chatti). They first enter the historical record in connection with Drusus' campaigns in Germania in 12–9 BC, and from that time onwards were periodically in conflict with the Romans. The most serious conflict was Domitian's war of 83, although we have very little information about it. The emphasis that Tacitus puts on the Chatti is probably a reflection of their importance in his day.

82. *let their hair ... enemy*: We can compare this with Tacitus' report that the Batavian leader Civilis took a 'barbarian vow' when he began his revolt against Rome, and did not cut his hair until he had defeated the Roman legions (*Hist.* 4.61.1); here he suggests that the Chatti turned this ad hoc practice into a general rite of passage. Since all Germani are regularly depicted in Roman sources with long hair and beards, it is not clear what would have distinguished these men in particular; most commentators suppose that their hair and beards were particularly unkempt.

83. *Usipi and Tencteri*: Caesar describes how in 55 BC these two groups (he calls the former by the alternative name Usipetes) crossed the lower Rhine into Gaul, where he inflicted a heavy defeat on them (*Gall.* 4.1 and 7–15). In 17 BC they crossed again, defeating the governor M. Lollius (Dio 54.20.4–6). Thereafter we hear of regular conflicts until the late first century AD, when the Usipi, at least, were enough under Roman control to serve as auxiliaries in the army; see *Agr.* 28 for an account of a famous mutiny. By the time of Tacitus both groups seem to have moved further south: the Usipi perhaps to the lower Lahn valley, the Tencteri somewhat to the north.

84. *the eldest*: The implication that the Germani practised primogeniture is out of keeping both with what Tacitus says above about inheritance (*Germ.* 20) and with later Germanic tradition; primogeniture is in fact not found until the high Middle Ages, and then only among the landed elite.

85. *Bructeri*: This people seems to have been among the most determined opponents of the Romans throughout the first century AD; they played a leading role in the revolt of Civilis, in part because of their influential seeress Veleda (Tac. *Hist.* 4.61.2; see further *Germ.* 8 with n. 25). They lived perhaps along the Lippe river.

86. *Chamavi ... Angrivarii*: There are few other references to either of these peoples, although the former seem to have maintained

their distinct identity into the fourth century (Ammianus
Marcellinus, *History* 17.8.5).

87. *battle*: Nothing else is known of this battle, although some scholars connect it to an episode mentioned by the younger Pliny, in
which a Roman general installed a king of the Bructeri in his
kingdom, and 'by threat of war overawed a particularly fierce
people' (*Ep.* 2.7.2); this probably took place in 97, shortly before
Tacitus wrote *Germania*.

88. *discord of our foes*: The interpretation of this sentence has been
much debated, especially the phrase *urgentibus imperii fatis*, translated here as 'the imperial destiny drives hard': is this destiny good
or bad? Many scholars, citing parallels from other Latin writers
(especially Livy 5.36.6 and 22.43.9), argue that it has a pessimistic
connotation: the Romans have so declined that their only hope
lies in their enemies' hostility to each other. Others, however, note
that there is little in the immediate context to suggest such a negative view, and argue that Tacitus simply meant the destiny of the
expanding empire. The debate has not been resolved.

89. *of no special note*: Evidently an accurate assessment, since there are
virtually no other references even to the Dulgubnii and Chasuarii.

90. *Frisii*: This people inhabited what is now the modern provinces
of Friesland and Groningen in the Netherlands. The Romans
first encountered them in 12 BC, when Drusus established an alliance with them (Dio 54.32.2–3). Thereafter they were normally
under Roman hegemony, although they effectively reasserted
their independence in 28 for a period of some twenty years (Tac.
Ann. 4.72–3 and 11.19) and took part in the revolt of Civilis
(Tac. *Hist.* 4.15.2). The 'vast lakes' were those in what is now the
area of the IJsselmeer and the reclaimed land around it (Mela
3.24, Plin. *NH* 4.101).

91. *pillars of ... Hercules*: By the 'pillars of Hercules', Tacitus probably
had in mind a supposed strait into the Ocean from the Caspian
Sea, comparable to the famous pillars of Hercules in the west (the
modern Straits of Gibraltar). Drusus (here given his posthumous
name Germanicus) was said to have been the first Roman to sail
the northern Ocean (Suet. *Claud.* 1.2). It was probably he, during his
campaigns of 12–9 BC, and not Tiberius in AD 5, as is often thought,
who was responsible for the expedition from the mouth of the
Rhine to the territory of the Cimbri in northern Jutland about
which Augustus boasted (*Achievements* 26.4; cf. Plin. *NH* 2.167).

92. *Chauci*: Drusus invaded their territory after his alliance with the
Frisii in 12 BC (Dio 54.32.2), and they seem to have maintained

some sort of allegiance to Rome as late as 16 (Tac. *Ann.* 2.17.5); by 41, however, we hear of a Roman campaign against them (Dio 60.8.7), and thereafter their relations with Rome were largely hostile.

93. *to the Chatti*: Several other sources refer to the Chauci as a coastal people, presumably east of the Frisii (Strabo 7.1.3, Plin. *NH* 16.2, Tac. *Ann.* 2.24.2), but none to their extending as far inland as the Chatti; if, however, the Cherusci had recently been wiped out (*Germ.* 36), the Chatti and Chauci may have taken over their former territory, so that Tacitus' account here would have reflected current conditions.

94. *never robbing ... neighbours*: No other source refers to the Chauci in these terms; in fact, Tacitus elsewhere mentions particular raids and attacks on other peoples (*Ann.* 11.18–19, 13.55.1).

95. *Cherusci ... victorious Chatti*: The Cherusci, who lived in the region of the Weser river, are best known as the people of Arminius, the leader of the Germanic ambush against Varus in 9 (see Introduction A3, and *Germ.* 37 with n. 102). Arminius was eventually killed by his own kinsmen (Tac. *Ann.* 2.88.2), which evidently led to a period of internal conflicts; in 47 the Cherusci had to appeal to Claudius to send as their king a nephew of Arminius who had grown up in Rome (Tac. *Ann.* 11.16–17). In the time of Domitian the Chatti expelled the Cheruscan king Chariomerus because of his alliance with Rome (Dio 67.5.1), which is probably the event to which Tacitus refers here. Since there are no later references to them, it probably marked the end of the Cherusci as an independent people.

96. *Cimbri*: Famous for their great migration in the late second century BC, in the course of which they inflicted major defeats on Rome and seemed on the verge of invading Italy, before being defeated by C. Marius; see Introduction A1, and nn. 101 and 103 below. About a century later, the Roman expedition under Drusus (see *Germ.* 34 with n. 91) encountered the Cimbri in their homeland in the north of Jutland, which ancient geographers called 'the promontory of the Cimbri' (Plin. *NH* 2.167, 4.96–7). It is unclear what led Drusus' men to identify this far distant people with the invaders of long ago; Strabo's story, that the Cimbri asked pardon for their earlier offences (7.2.1), is inherently implausible.

97. *two hundred and ten years*: C. Caecilius Metellus and Cn. Papirius Carbo were consuls in 113 BC, and Trajan's second consulship was in 98; Tacitus' reference to the latter provides our only solid evidence for the date of *Germania*.

98. *more painful lessons*: Tacitus here lists some of the major enemies of Rome. The Samnites, a people of central Italy, fought a series of wars with Rome from the mid fourth to the early third century BC. The Punic Wars between Rome and the North African city of Carthage extended from the mid third to the mid second century BC. Rome began its conquest of Hispania in the late third century BC, but did not complete it until the end of the first century BC. For Roman wars with the Gauls, see Introduction A1. The Parthians, the major power in what is now Iraq and Iran, were the great rivals of Rome in the East from the mid first century BC until well after the time of Tacitus.

99. *Arsaces*: The founder of the royal house of the Parthians. This sentence provides the central idea of this long and detailed chapter, which is in turn central to *Germania* as a whole; see Introduction D2.

100. *Crassus ... Ventidius*: M. Licinius Crassus, the ally and rival of Caesar and Pompey, launched a major assault against the Parthians in 54 BC, only to be killed in a massacre at Carrhae the following year. In 41–40 BC, the Parthian prince Pacorus led an army into Roman territory, but was killed two years later by the Roman general P. Ventidius Bassus.

101. *five consular armies*: Generals defeated by the Cimbri and their allies: Cn. Papirius Carbo in 113 BC; L. Cassius Longinus in 107 BC; M. Aurelius Scaurus, Q. Servilius Caepio and Cn. Mallius Maximus, all in 105 BC. Tacitus speaks a little loosely, since neither Scaurus nor Caepio were consuls at the time of their defeat.

102. *Caesar ... three legions*: By 'Caesar', Tacitus here means Augustus. P. Quinctilius Varus was the chief Roman commander in Germania in 7–9. In 9, the Cheruscan leaders Arminius and Segimerus, who had won his confidence, secretly organized an ambush at the Teutoburg Forest and massacred the three legions under his command; Varus himself committed suicide (Vell. Pat. 2.117–19, Dio 56.18–22). Augustus observed the anniversary of the battle as a day of mourning (Suet. *Aug.* 23). Its site has recently been identified at Kalkriese near Osnabrück.

103. *C. Marius ... in their own lands*: Tacitus balances the list of Roman defeats with a list of Roman victories. Marius defeated the Cimbri and their allies in a series of major battles in 102 and 101 BC; Julius Caesar engaged with Germanic peoples a number of times during his conquest of Gaul, most notably with those under Ariovistus in 58 BC. Drusus campaigned in Germania in

12–9 BC, Tiberius (here called by his original cognomen Nero) in 8–7 BC, AD 4–6 and 10–11, Germanicus in 14–16. Although there must have been Roman losses on all these occasions, only in connection with Germanicus' campaigns in 15 do we hear of any serious problems (Tac. *Ann.* 1.63–8); Tacitus' point is thus more rhetorical than strictly accurate.

104. *ended in farce*: A contemptuous reference to Gaius' campaign of 39–40; see *Agr.* 13 with n. 43.

105. *claim possession of Gaul*: A reference to the revolt of the Batavi under C. Julius Civilis, which began amidst the civil wars of 69 and was finally put down in 70 by Vespasian's general Q. Petilius Cerialis (Tac. *Hist.* 4.12–37 and 54–79, 5.14–26; Josephus, *Jewish War* 7.75–88). The statement that Germani claimed possession of Gaul is at odds with Tacitus' more detailed account in *The Histories*; there, after Civilis incites the Gallic Treveri and Lingones to revolt, they attempt to establish an 'empire of the Gauls', independent of the Germanic peoples who follow Civilis.

106. *more with triumphs than with victories*: A barbed allusion to Domitian's much-mocked triumph over the Chatti in 83; see *Agr.* 39 with n. 91.

107. *all alike are called Suebi*: The name 'Suebi' is Germanic, although its precise meaning has been much disputed. Roman writers used the term in very different ways in different periods: those of the latter half of the first century BC applied it to a single people pushing westwards across the Rhine; those of the first century AD applied it to a number of separate peoples along the Elbe. The connection between the two probably lies in the Marcomanic leader Maroboduus' migration eastwards and his subsequent rule over a number of peoples in that region (*Germ.* 42 with nn. 118 and 120). Tacitus here applies the name to all the Germanic peoples who, from the Roman point of view, lived beyond the Danube as opposed to the Rhine. There is little reason to think, however, that his categorization had much basis in reality; the only distinctively 'Suebian' feature that he notes is a hairstyle, but even that is uncertain (see the following note).

108. *with a knot*: This hairstyle is well attested. Other Roman writers describe it as typical of the Germani (Seneca, *On Wrath* 3.26.3; Juv. 13.164–5), it often appears in Roman visual depictions of Germani, and it has been found on a few of the so-called 'bog bodies'. Tacitus, however, is the only source that associates it specifically with the Suebi.

109. *among the Suebi ... twisted back*: There is a problem with the text of this sentence; the translation given here is simply an attempt to make some sense of it.

110. *Semnones*: A people who apparently lived east of the middle Elbe, often described as Suebi by Greek and Roman writers. They were one of the peoples over whom Maroboduus established his rule (Strabo 7.1.3), but later deserted him for Arminius (Tac. *Ann.* 2.45.1). Their king, Masyus, visited Domitian (Dio 67.5.3), perhaps in connection with that emperor's war against the Marcomani (see *Germ.* 42 with n. 118); Masyus was perhaps the source of these claims about the Semnones' pre-eminence among the Suebi.

111. *there the god is ruler of all*: The Latin phrase *ibi regnator omnium deus* is often translated as 'there is the god who is ruler of all', leading to much speculation about the identity of this supreme Germanic deity; Woden has been the most favoured candidate. But it is more likely simply to mean that the god was regarded as the absolute ruler of the grove, and this is how I have translated it here.

112. *Langobardi*: The name, obviously Germanic, means 'Long-beards'. Their homeland seems to have been in the area south of present-day Hamburg. Like the Semnones, they are often identified as Suebi (Strabo 7.1.3), were originally under the rule of Maroboduus and deserted him for Arminius (Tac. *Ann.* 2.45.1). In the late sixth century they established a kingdom in northern Italy, what is now Lombardy. The eighth-century Lombard writer Paul the Deacon wrote a history of his people that preserves many native traditions, including the story that they originated in Scandinavia.

113. *Reudigni ... Nuitones*: None of these peoples is definitely attested in other ancient sources, although the Varini might be identical with the Varinnae of Pliny (see n. 7 above). The Anglii were to become famous after their invasion of Britannia at the end of the fifth century; their homeland at that time was evidently the modern region of Angeln in northeastern Schleswig.

114. *Nerthus, or Mother Earth*: This is the only reference anywhere to this cult. We can perhaps connect Tacitus' description of her cart with two elaborately decorated carts found in a bog in Jutland, which are likely to have been reserved for ritual use; we can perhaps also connect the name 'Nerthus' with that of Njorthr, who in early Norse myth is the father of the fertility god Freyr (although Njorthr himself seems more associated

with seafaring). But Tacitus' description of this cult has obviously been shaped to some extent by his familiarity with the cult of the Roman goddess the Great Mother; it is thus difficult to be sure how reliable it is.

115. *Hermunduri*: The location of this people is uncertain, since references to them are inconsistent. Some scholars associate their name with that of Thuringia (seeing '-duri' as equivalent to 'Thur-'). Such a location would fit well with reports that associate them with the Marcomani in what is now the Czech Republic (Tac. *Ann.* 2.63.5, 12.29.1). On the other hand, Tacitus' assertion that they came to trade in Augusta Vindelicum (see the following note) suggests a location much closer to the Danube. No other source emphasizes their loyalty to Rome as Tacitus does here, or mentions their special trading privileges.

116. *illustrious colony ... Raetia*: Tacitus presumably means Augusta Vindelicum (mod. Augsburg), the provincial capital, even though it was not at this time a Roman colony.

117. *famous river ... by name alone*: The Elbe rises in the mountains on what is now the northwest border of the Czech Republic, far from where Tacitus seems to locate the Hermunduri; but he may have identified the main stream of the Elbe as the Saale, which rises in the southern part of Thuringia. During the attempted conquest of Germania under Augustus, Roman armies repeatedly reached the Elbe: under Drusus in 9 BC (Dio 55.1.2), under L. Domitius Ahenobarbus in 7 and 2 BC (Dio 55.10a.2, Tac. *Ann.* 4.44.2) and under Tiberius in 5 (Vell. Pat. 2.106.2–3, Dio 55.28.5). Tacitus' pointed comment is aimed at the decline of Roman ambitions in Germania.

118. *Naristi ... Quadi*: There are relatively few references to the Naristi and Quadi, most of which associate them in some way with the Marcomani (later spelled with a double 'n', which has become standard in modern discussions). The latter probably originated in the region of the Elbe, but were among the peoples who pushed west under Ariovistus (Caes. *Gall.* 1.51.2), and apparently settled along the upper Main; it was perhaps as a result that they received their name of 'March-Men', i.e., inhabitants of a border region. After being defeated by Drusus, they moved into Bohemia under the leadership of Maroboduus (see n. 120 below). Thereafter they maintained good relations with Rome until the late 80s, when Domitian initiated a war against them (Dio 67.7.1–2); in 97 there was further trouble, resulting in a victory for Nerva (Plin. *Pan.* 8.2).

119. *drove out the Boii*: See *Germ.* 28 with n. 72.

120. *depend upon the authority of Rome*: A number of Marcomanic kings are known from the first century AD, and the evidence suggests that Rome played an important, if often indirect, role in their selection. The most important of them was Maroboduus, who according to Strabo spent some time as a young man in Rome; after leading the Marcomani in their migration to Bohemia, he acquired authority over a number of other peoples, including the Semnones and the Lugii (Strabo 7.1.3). In 17, Arminius, having failed to win his support for the war against Rome, mounted a successful attack, resulting in Maroboduus' loss of control over all his subjects except the Marcomani (Tac. *Ann.* 2.44–6); two years later, he was expelled in a coup, and spent the last twenty years of his life at Ravenna (Tac. *Ann.* 2.62–3). Nothing else is known of Tudrus.

121. *Marsigni, Cotini, Osi and Buri*: There are few other references to any of these peoples, although the Cotini and Buri are mentioned in connection with the Marcomanic wars of the 170s; they perhaps lived in the area of what is now Slovakia. For the Osi, see also *Germ.* 28 with n. 73.

122. *mine iron*: In the Roman empire, most of the labour for mining operations was provided by slaves and condemned criminals; hence the shame that Tacitus attributes to this activity.

123. *unbroken range of mountains*: Probably the mountains that lie on the current border between the Czech Republic and Slovakia to the south and Germany and Poland to the north.

124. *Lugii ... Nahanarvali*: Tacitus seems to locate the Lugii in the general region of modern Silesia. They were one of the peoples under the rule of Maroboduus (Strabo 7.1.3), but after his downfall seem to have had mostly hostile relations with the Marcomani. Ptolemy also mentions several branches of the Lugii (2.10.10), although his list of names has little overlap with that given here; otherwise, there are no other references to these specific peoples (the name Nahanarvali appears in some manuscripts as Naharvali, which certain editors prefer). Some commentators want to identify Tacitus' Lugii with Pliny's Vandili (*NH* 4.99), but there is little to associate the two groups apart from the fact that they are both said to comprise various subgroups.

125. *young men and brothers*: Cults of divine twins are attested in a number of Indo-European cultures, not only Greek (Castor and Pollux), but also Indo-Iranian and Baltic; this is the best evidence that such a cult existed in Germanic culture as well. The name

'Alci' has been variously interpreted: some link it to Gothic *alhs*, 'temple', others to Old English *ealgian*, 'to protect', and still others to the Germanic word *alces*, 'elks', recorded by Caesar (*Gall.* 6.27.1). Greek and Latin writers normally translated foreign divine names into the closest Graeco-Roman equivalent; modern scholars, borrowing Tacitus' phrase here, conventionally describe this practice as *interpretatio Romana*, 'Roman translation'.

126. *Gotones*: There are few other references to this people in ancient writers; Ptolemy (3.5.8) locates them near the Vistula, apparently to the north of modern Warsaw, and Pliny describes them (under the name 'Gutones') as one of the peoples who make up the Vandili (n. 7 above). Otherwise, we know only that they harboured the Marcomanic fugitive Catualda, who successfully went on to challenge Maroboduus for the kingship (Tac. *Ann.* 2.62.2; see n. 120 above). They are often identified with the later Goths.

127. *Rugii ... Lemovii*: No other writer mentions the Rugii until the fifth century, when they established a kingdom on the middle Danube; the Lemovii are otherwise unknown.

128. *Suiones, amidst the Ocean itself*: 'Suiones' is clearly a Latinized form of the name that later appears as Old English *Swéon* and Old Norse *Svíar*, that is, the Swedes; there are no other clear references to this people until the sixth century. The meaning of the phrase *ipso in Oceano*, here translated 'amidst the Ocean itself', is not entirely certain, but Tacitus probably meant that they lived on an island. It is interesting to compare a passage of the elder Pliny (*NH* 4.96; cf. Mela 3.54), who describes a great northern island that is called 'Scadinavia'(*sic*) and is inhabited by the 'Hilleviones'; some people have argued that the latter is a corruption of *ille Suiones*, 'those Suiones', which would match Tacitus' report here.

129. *The shape ... side to side*: Actual examples of ancient Scandinavian boats recovered from bogs conform very closely to Tacitus' description: the earliest of these has steering oars at both ends and lacks both mast and rowlocks.

130. *sluggish and almost immobile*: See *Agr.* 10 with n. 32.

131. *Only ... extend*: There is a problem with the text of this sentence, but the general sense was probably along the lines given here.

132. *Aestii*: Usually identified with the ancient Balts, the forerunners of the modern Lithuanians and Latvians, because of their location and association with amber. By the 'Suebian Sea' (the term is found only here) Tacitus presumably means the Baltic, and by

'the right-hand shore' the territory extending from old East Prussia to Latvia, the historical homeland of Baltic-speaking peoples. The notion that their language was closer to the Celtic language of Britannia must be mistaken.

133. *amber – glesum is their own word for it*: Glesum (see also Plin. *NH* 37.42) is in fact clearly a Germanic word, related to English 'glass', suggesting either that the Aestii were Germanic speaking or, more likely, that the Romans learned the word from Germanic middlemen. Amber was the most prized import from northern Europe into the Mediterranean, and the amber trade between the two regions can be traced back as early as *c.* 1600 BC. According to Pliny, the Romans originally acquired amber from Germani along the Danube, but in the reign of Nero an enterprising merchant acquired a supply on his own (*NH* 37.44–6); this may reflect the establishment of a direct trade route that bypassed Germanic middlemen and led to Roman familiarity with the Aestii.

134. *Sitones*: No other writer mentions this people. Since Tacitus has already said that beyond the Suiones there is nothing but the sluggish sea, it is now odd that he returns to them and locates another people in their vicinity.

135. *Peucini … Bastarnae*: Other writers also associated these two peoples, although in different ways: Strabo (7.3.17) describes the Peucini as a subgroup of the Bastarnae, whom he locates inland from the Black Sea, between the Danube and the Dnieper; Pliny (*NH* 4.100) says that the Bastarnae and Peucini together make up one of the major groupings of Germani. Greek evidence indicates that the Bastarnae moved into the area of the Black Sea as early as the late third century BC; fifty years later they served as allies of the Macedonian kings in their wars with Rome (Polybius, *History* 25.6.2–6). In the first century BC they twice crossed the Danube into Thrace, and on the second occasion were defeated by the Romans (Dio 51.23–4). Polybius and other early sources classify them as Gauls; later sources tend, like Tacitus here, to associate them with the Sarmatians.

136. *Veneti*: This name appears in other writers as Venedae. Pliny (*NH* 4.97) locates them near the Vistula; Ptolemy (3.5.7) lists them, along with the Peucini and the Bastarnae, among the major peoples of Sarmatia. Their identification is very uncertain; later Germanic speakers applied the name to the Slavic-speaking peoples east of the Elbe (German *Wenden*), but it is impossible to say whether that has any bearing on these earlier reports.

137. *Fenni*: Versions of this name appear in writers of the sixth century and later, who seem to use it of the Lapps. In Tacitus' day there were certainly sub-Neolithic peoples living in northern Scandinavia and the eastern Baltic, and some second-hand report about a people like this probably lies behind his account here.

138. *Hellusii ... Oxiones*: Neither name appears anywhere else, but stories of fantastic races at the edge of the earth were common currency in antiquity; see, for example, Mela 3.56 and Plin. *NH* 4.95.

Index of Personal Names

References are to sections of the Introduction, chapters of *Agricola* and *Germania* (distinguished by **bold** type) and to the notes on *Agricola* and *Germania*. Dates are AD unless specified otherwise.

Index of Peoples and Places

This index includes all references to peoples and places in the texts themselves, as well as significant discussions in the Introduction and notes; chapters of *Agricola* and *Germania* are distinguished by **bold** type. Dates are AD unless specified otherwise.

PENGUIN CLASSICS

THE RISE OF THE ROMAN EMPIRE
POLYBIUS

> 'If history is deprived of the truth,
> we are left with nothing but an idle, unprofitable tale'

In writing his account of the relentless growth of the Roman Empire, the Greek statesman Polybius (*c.* 200–118 BC) set out to help his fellow-countrymen understand how their world came to be dominated by Rome. Opening with the Punic War in 264 BC, he vividly records the critical stages of Roman expansion: its campaigns throughout the Mediterranean, the temporary setbacks inflicted by Hannibal and the final destruction of Carthage in 146 BC. An active participant in contemporary politics, as well as a friend of many prominent Roman citizens, Polybius was able to draw on a range of eyewitness accounts and on his own experiences of many of the central events, giving his work immediacy and authority.

Ian Scott-Kilvert's translation fully preserves the clarity of Polybius' narrative. This substantial selection of the surviving volumes is accompanied by an introduction by F. W. Walbank, which examines Polybius' life and times, and the sources and technique he employed in writing his history.

Translated by Ian Scott-Kilvert
Selected with an introduction by F. W. Walbank

PENGUIN CLASSICS

THE ANNALS OF IMPERIAL ROME
TACITUS

'Nero was already corrupted by every lust, natural and unnatural'

The Annals of Imperial Rome recount the major historical events from the years shortly before the death of Augustus to the death of Nero in AD 68. With clarity and vivid intensity Tacitus describes the reign of terror under the corrupt Tiberius, the great fire of Rome during the time of Nero and the wars, poisonings, scandals, conspiracies and murders that were part of imperial life. Despite his claim that the *Annals* were written objectively, Tacitus' account is sharply critical of the emperors' excesses and fearful for the future of imperial Rome, while also filled with a longing for its past glories.

Michael Grant's fine translation captures the moral tone, astringent wit and stylish vigour of the original. His introduction discusses the life and works of Tacitus and the historical context of the *Annals*. This edition also contains a key to place names and technical terms, maps, tables and suggestions for further reading.

Translated with an introduction by Michael Grant

Penguin Classics

THE REPUBLIC
PLATO

'We are concerned with the most important of issues, the choice between a good and an evil life'

Plato's *Republic* is widely acknowledged as the cornerstone of Western philosophy. Presented in the form of a dialogue between Socrates and three different interlocutors, it is an inquiry into the notion of a perfect community and the ideal individual within it. During the conversation other questions are raised: what is goodness; what is reality; what is knowledge? *The Republic* also addresses the purpose of education and the roles of both women and men as 'guardians' of the people. With remarkable lucidity and deft use of allegory, Plato arrives at a depiction of a state bound by harmony and ruled by 'philosopher kings'.

Desmond Lee's translation of *The Republic* has come to be regarded as a classic in its own right. The new introduction by Melissa Lane discusses Plato's aims in writing *The Republic*, its major arguments and perspective on politics in ancient Greece, and its significance through the ages and today.

Translated with an introduction by Desmond Lee